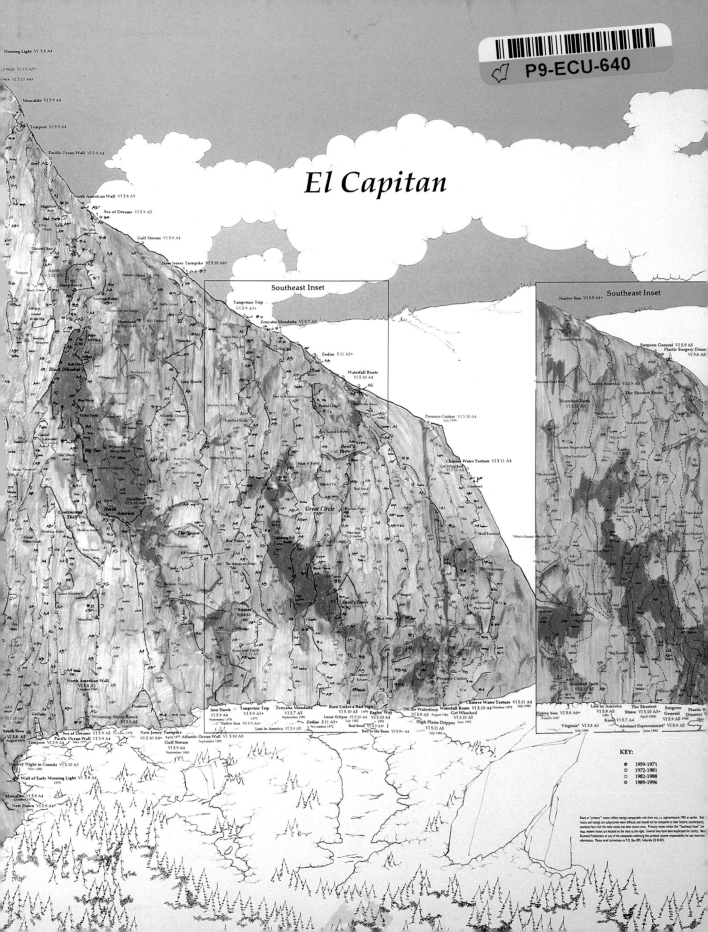

el capitan

el capitan

historic feats and radical routes

by Daniel Duane

CHRONICLE BOOKS

SAN FRANCISCO

Acknowledgments: This is only *a* book about El Cap, by no means *the* book about El Cap. I am not a historian by trade, and made no attempt to recount every important climb in the wall's history, nor to talk to an all-inclusive group of climbers. The climbers with whom I did speak, however, were uniformly forthcoming and generous with their time. For that reason, this small book would have been impossible without the gracious and unrewarded help of "Big Wall" Amy Aucoin, Werner Braun, Chris Breemer, Jim Bridwell, Scott Burk, Ed Cooper, Mike Corbett, Mike Davis, Roger Derryberry, Hans Florine, Tom Frost, Steve Gerberding, Warren Harding, Jonathan Kaplan, Mary Lou Long, Rick Lovelace, Chris McNamara, Peter Mayfield, John Middendorf, Royal Robbins, Charlie Row, Steve Schneider, Allen Steck, and Mark Wellman. Special thanks to Kelly Duane for photoediting. Apologies to anyone I have forgotten to thank. Lastly, I wish, right now, to give credit to my sources for whatever is good about this book, and to claim the blame for whatever factual inaccuracies it may contain.

Library of Congress Cataloging-in-Publication Data available.

ISBN 0-8118-2484-5
Printed in Hong Kong.

Designed by Meryl Pollen

Distributed in Canada by Raincoast Books
9050 Shaughnessy Street, Vancouver, British Columbia V6P 6E5

10 9 8 7 6 5 4 3 2 1

Chronicle Books LLC
85 Second Street, San Francisco, California 94105
www.chroniclebooks.com

page 2: El Capitan.

FOR TOM FROST AND MY FATHER, RICHARD DUANE, AND FOR CAMP 4

contents

following spread: Gear Selection, second ascent, the Nose.

"So it happens that the wealthier and more advanced a society, the more fanatic its interest in certain kinds of sport. Civilization's trajectory is to curve back upon itself—naturally? Helplessly?—like the mythical snake biting its own tail and to take up with passion the outward signs and gestures of "savagery." While it is plausible that emotionally effete men and women may require ever more extreme experiences to arouse them, it is perhaps the case too that the desire is not merely to *mimic* but, magically, to *be* brute, primitive, instinctive, and therefore innocent. One might then be a person for whom the contest is not mere self-destructive play but life itself; and the world, not in spectacular and irrevocable decline, but new, fresh, vital, terrifying and exhilarating by turns, a place of wonders."

Joyce Carol Oates, ON BOXING

"Everything painful and sobering in what psychoanalytic genius and religious genius have discovered about man revolves around the terror of admitting what one is doing to earn his self-esteem. This is why human heroics is a blind drivenness that burns people up; in passionate people, a screaming for glory is as uncritical and reflexive as the howling of a dog."

Ernest Becker, THE DENIAL OF DEATH

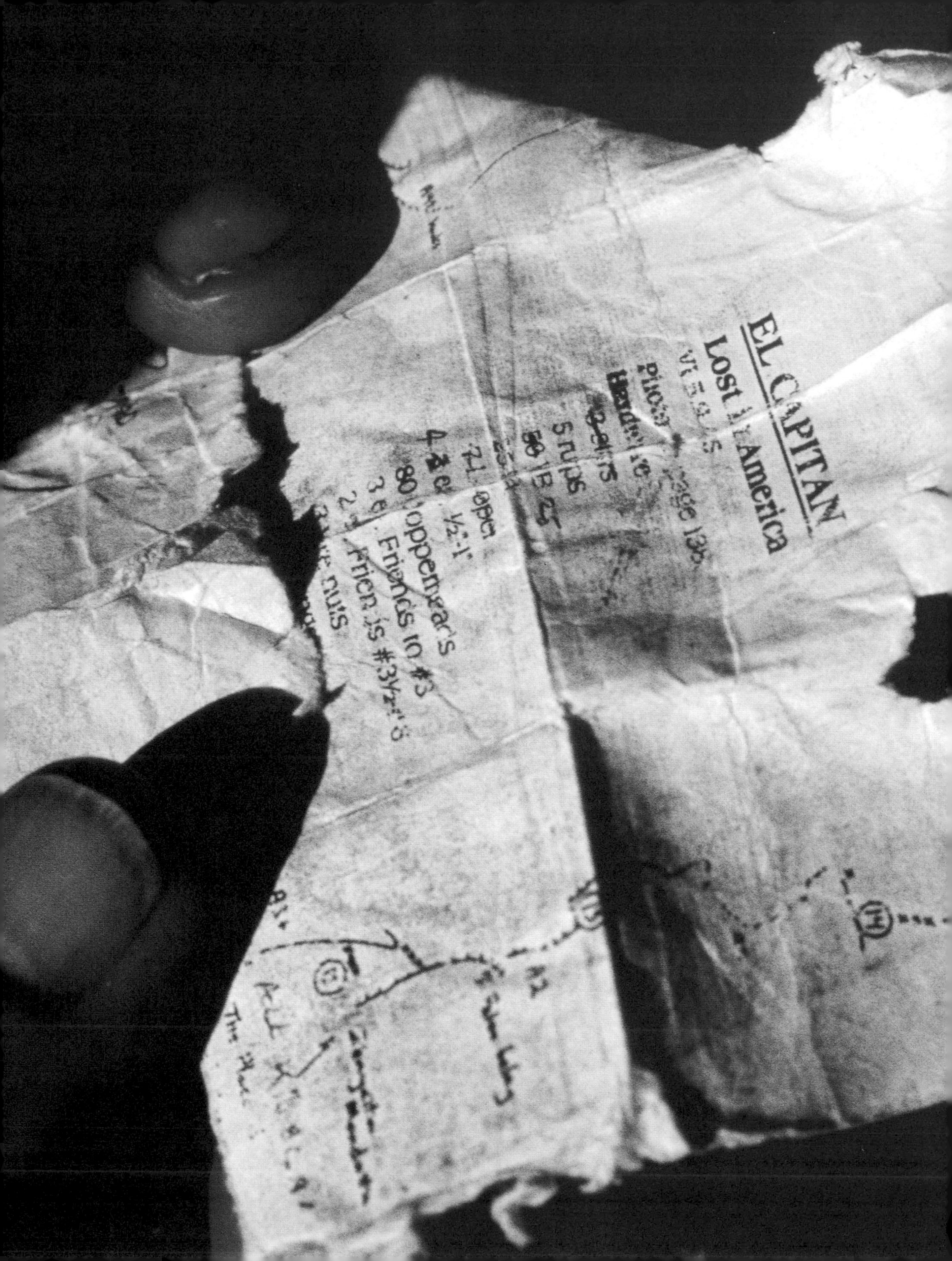
EL CAPITAN

There was a time—two full years, in fact—
when climbing the 3000-foot
sheer granite monolith called El Capitan meant literally everything to me. I was in my early twenties and had somehow gotten it through my head that El Capitan lay as a kind of obstacle to the rest of my life—that I couldn't get on with becoming whoever I was supposed to become until I had thrashed my way up the thing. My parents and my friends all knew this, and they regularly told me that they wouldn't like me any less one way or another—hoping, I suppose, to defuse my potentially dangerous obsession. They even pointed out that, statistically speaking, one hundred percent of humanity led lives in no way dependent upon their having climbed or not climbed El Capitan (or anything else, for that matter), and surely I could find less hazardous ways of proving myself. None of this meant a thing. My internal apparatus of desire and ambition had simply built itself around this single object; I knew without a shred of a doubt that if I failed to climb El Capitan, I would live my entire life in an intractable fog of doubt and self-loathing.

I got myself into this predicament by accepting wholeheartedly, at about the age of nineteen, what might be called the Path of the Yosemite Climber. Somewhat out of vogue now, in this era of bolt-clipping gym climbers, and never more than a tacit understanding between Valley regulars, this path is simply a sequence of rock climbs, beginning with practice routes and proceeding through several years' worth of progressively harder ascents. "Do these five 5.9 climbs in good style," the story goes, "and you can then begin to consider trying that one 5.10. Put the following ten 5.10s behind you,

TOPO, Lost in America.

without falls, and you might deign to call yourself a 5.10 climber." For anyone who wants a path to self-knowledge, or adventure, or enlightenment, or whatever it is that we want such paths for, this makes a brilliant one, complete with seasonal movements from the short, winter training climbs of Joshua Tree, to Yosemite in the spring, up to Tuolumne Meadows for the hot months of summer, and then back to Yosemite for the autumnal big wall season.

You start out by following other climbers, learning to remove protective gear from the rock, and then you take your first lead on something short and easy, allowing plenty of time to fiddle with the equipment. Then the leads get harder and longer and months and whole summers pass in the comfort of this meaningful march forward. Along the way, you probably try a few of the short climbs at the base of El Cap, like Moby Dick, and you feel the stone's absurd stature, its staggering, elemental size—as if you've put your hands on the side of a planet. Three years in and you're ticking off the long, single-day routes, thrashing your way up the finger and fist cracks, squeeze-chimneys and slabs of the Valley's pure granite walls, tasting the remarkable pleasure of running fast over stone all day. Finishing late in the day, you thrill to another of the Valley's peculiar joys: the long, long walk down, stumbling in the warm night through the trees, laughing with the climber's utterly unique brand of elation, a mysterious and giddy delight at things meaningful simply because they are possible. What I have done today, you can't help feeling, makes no sense, and yet it has made me extraordinarily happy.

Rest days pass swimming in the crystal clear pools of the Merced River, sunning on midstream boulders, watching trout flickering here and there. Maybe an ice cream at the deli and a long nap in the tall, wind-whispering grasses of El Cap meadow, sleeping with the peace of physical well-being. Over time, as you lie day after day down there looking up, picking out tiny climbers lost in their dreams, you begin to realize where all this is going. An elaborate oral history has crept into your thoughts through the osmosis of parking-lot conversations, all about the Valley's own pantheon of gods and demi-gods, great achievements, disasters, and debates—how Warren Harding got mobbed by biting ants on the first ascent of that one-day route you just loved so thoroughly, and how Royal Robbins did the first ascent of Half Dome in 1957, when he was only twenty-one years old. Harding's two-year siege of the Nose of El Capitan seems only testimony to the wall's unimaginable vastness, and you pass hours picking out the climb's famous features: Sickle Ledge, the Stoveleg Cracks, Dolt Tower, Boot Flake, the Great Roof. Robbins's nine-day first ascent of El Cap's next route, the Salathé, with Tom Frost and Chuck Pratt, seems an act of wizardry, and his North America Wall, with Frost, Pratt, and Yvon Chouinard, to the right, seems pure genius—inscribing El Capitan, as that route does, with continental significance. Even the old ethical arguments loom like scriptural debates between apostles: to bolt or not to bolt? How shall we, as a people, define what we call right and wrong? The faces from the photographs become likewise etched into your mind. From Yosemite's golden age, it's mostly Harding, the swarthy, Byronesque wise cracker, and Robbins, the bespectacled fanatic; also funny T. M. Herbert, gear-master and philosopher Yvon Chouinard, sprightly Tom

following spread: Iron.

Frost and stocky, implacable Chuck Pratt. From the weirder, wilder 1970s, it's all about Jim Bridwell, the man who pushed Robbins's continental metaphor to the next level, establishing Pacific Ocean Wall in the blank sweeps to the left of the black diorite known as North America, and then set an altogether new standard for boldness and commitment with his still-terrifying Sea of Dreams, harder than anything the pioneers had attempted. Perhaps, if you were paying attention as hard as I was, you knew that even in the 1980s hard new routes were going up all over El Cap, and you tried to catch sight of Rick Lovelace or John Middendorf in the cafeteria, wondered what insane aid wall they'd just come off.

All of it argues for the primacy of the wall you know you've got to climb next: El Capitan, naturally, the sine qua non of a Yosemite climbing career. Remember that this is only one version of a path that many climbers would say doesn't exist, and that there are taller cliffs in the world, such as those on the Trango Towers of the Karakoram Himalaya and on Baffin Island, all with far more fearsome weather and rockfall potential than El Capitan. No wall on earth, however, drops quite so sheer and smooth in such a perfect vertical sweep of solid granite as does El Capitan, from a flat top to a ninety-degree plummet into the soil, nor in such a sunny clime so close to a road and a bar and a very big audience. The effect of that stone's scale and singularity is so great that groups of tourists routinely gather in the meadow below simply to stare at the thing, using binoculars and high-powered telescopes to pick out climbers as if searching the skies for lost astronauts. Indeed, the first recorded white sighting of the wall comes from a U.S. Cavalry doctor who rode into the valley in 1851, got one look at El Capitan, and fell behind his regiment to sit staring upwards in awe, his heart pounding and his eyes filling with tears. When another soldier called back to the doctor, worried there might be scalping Indians in the trees, the doctor replied that "If my hair is now required, I can depart in peace, for I have here seen the power and glory of a Supreme being."

• • •

In my fourth summer of rockclimbing, in 1991, I tried and failed to climb El Capitan three times. The first time, on Warren Harding's Nose route with my friend Reuben Margolin, I was overcome by terror while still relatively low on the wall. The wall seemed impossibly vast, towering overhead with winds running almost constantly along the face, and birds rose and fell in dramatic demonstrations of gravity; hour upon hour of crushing physical labor brought the summit not an inch closer even as the ground got frighteningly far away. Then, while only half-way through the classic first day's work, I traversed onto a part of the wall on which the exposure—meaning the vertical drop below, the sheer volume of wall and space swimming all around—preyed upon the stability of my mind. My thoughts began to swirl about uncontrollably and I felt a terrible, inchoate urgency, as if something absolutely had to be done, and very, very soon. So I did something: I went down. The second failure, with my college climbing partner Jonathan Kaplan, came on the third day, when I dropped a bag containing rain gear and warm

clothing, and refused to go any farther—forcing us into nearly 2000 feet of rappels. My third failure was much like the first. My partner that time, Russ McBride, was so unafraid at belays that even as we dangled in the Stoveleg Cracks, he kept right on reading *One Hundred and One No Down Payment Formulas: How to Get Rich Quick in the Real Estate Market*. I was, however, utterly and desperately terrified once again. (I actually wept with fear, babbling incoherently about how I loved my mother and wanted to live to get married and have babies of my own someday.)

The following summer, I enlisted both Reuben and Jonathan on a fourth attempt. The idea was to have the strength of both men and also to resolve the debts I felt to them. We spent five and a half days on the Salathé Wall, and it was unquestionably the single greatest adventure of my life—sleeping on small ledges high in space, dangling on ropes from overhanging headwalls, and living day after day inside the security of total purpose. The quotidian world was always visible below, with the RVs and buses and cars, the crowds of tourists in their lawn chairs in the meadow, but it was so distant, as if we were proper fools on the hill. The fear was still there, a perpetual background hum of abject horror, but at least I knew where I was coming from, where I was going, and what I was supposed to do with myself. A hard-hat construction worker once told me that a day of big wall climbing is harder than any day on any job site. The climbing itself, the endless coiling of ropes and switching of equipment, the hours and hours of awkward body positions, hauling hundred-pound supply loads and ascending ropes, exposure to the elements and the yawning maw of space below—it all wears you down

North America Wall.

relentlessly. (Todd Skinner has said that you get so high up there on El Cap that when you look down it takes five minutes to see the ground.) A love for the sport, therefore, is a love of extreme physical discomfort and a hunger for jobs so stupidly difficult they can obliterate your self—the ostensible point of the whole enterprise.

So, having worked hard from dawn until dusk for nearly a week, having been literally shit upon by climbers high above us, cleansed by a warm summer rain, and buzzed by peregrine falcons, we neared the summit badly sunburnt, many pounds skinnier, and covered in filth and scabs and open wounds; profoundly exhausted and also very, very happy in the way of tired and healthy young animals. Then I discovered that there were depths of obsession with this wall that made my own look like a passing summer fancy. Far off to one side of the great cliff, we were arranging the short rappels back to the ground via the standard East Ledges descent route. Old, frayed ropes hung from bolts in the rock at our feet clear to the level terrain several hundred feet below us: "fixed lines" used by Yosemite Search and Rescue to access quickly the rim of El Capitan. Where the ropes had worn dangerously thin, they had simply been cut through and tied in knots. Having survived nearly a week in a purely vertical world, with the threat of death by falling everpresent, we had no intention of trusting our lives to such ephemera. For this reason, I spent several minutes rigging a heavily redundant anchor while Jonathan coiled and tossed our ropes off the edge, establishing our own rappel line. Reuben, meanwhile, readied our two enormous haul bags—the plasticized duffel sacks in which we'd carried our two hundred pounds of food, water, clothing, and bivouac gear. We were just about to descend when we heard footsteps.

Three men appeared, breathing hard and moving fast. One, I had seen before in Tuolumne Meadows. A mountaineering guide and rock-climbing instructor, he often wore a broad-brimmed Stetson while out with clients, and he had the wiry, efficient build of a cowhand. The second was rounder of body, with a gentle face and friendly smile, while the third was tall and lanky, his brown hair an unkempt, curly bush, and his mustache drawn down the sides of his mouth. In a very polite manner, this last asked if we would mind their rappelling ahead of us.

"We've just been moving for kind of a long time," he said, apologetically, "and if we stop now, we're going to fall asleep. Don't worry," he added with a grin, "we'll be real fast."

I deferred, and watched in astonishment as the climbing instructor started down the fixed lines. When he reached a knot in the rope, he simply held on to the rope with one hand, unclipped his rappel device with the other, reattached the rappel device below the knot, and continued on his way—his entire life held, for that minute or so, in the palm of his hand. Reuben, Jonathan, and I exchanged amazed glances: Who were these guys?

"What you boys been on?" asked the man with the mustache, now seated beside me on the ground. He had flinty, bright eyes, a winning smile, and an air of silent confidence. He was one of those rare men whose alpha status seems to emanate from their pores, their rank in any group somehow implicit, beyond question.

following spread: Zodiac belay.

"Salathé," I said, perhaps a little proudly.

"Oh, that's awesome," he replied. "I've always wanted to do that route. Your first El Cap route?"

I allowed that it was.

"Right on. You guys must be feeling great. How long were you up there?"

"Five days," I told him, although in truth it had been closer to six. It's just that five sounded like the upper end of respectable for that route, where six was starting to be a little hapless.

"Right on," he said. "Congratulations. I've *got* to do the Salathé some day. Is it just great?"

"It's amazing," I told him, only unconsciously catching the cue, the way his intonation of "Salathé" implied that he had done many, many other El Cap routes. "It was my fourth try, though," I confessed.

"Doesn't even matter," the man assured me. "Everybody bails a few times. What matters is you made it. You ticked it."

"I guess so." I smiled. I guessed I'd ticked it. That sounded good. "What'd you guys just do?" I asked.

"Mescalito," the man replied.

If the Salathé was one of the three great pioneering routes on El Capitan, Mescalito belonged in my mind to the same family as Pacific Ocean Wall and Sea of Dreams, climbs so committing they could apparently do dangerous and unsettling things to your mind. Much harder and steeper than the Salathé, Mescalito seemed far beyond a Rubicon I would never cross. I hadn't even made it back to the car yet, and my mental conversation could no longer

Ed Cooper, first ascent, Dihedral Wall.

revolve around simply having climbed El Cap. Already, I was in the realm of *Which route?*

But then I noticed something, and asked: "Where's your haul bag?"

"We didn't really bring one," he replied, "just that thing." He pointed to a sack about a third the size of ours.

"How long were you up there?"

"Twenty-eight hours," the man replied.

Twenty-eight hours.

"One guy climbing the whole time."

Twenty-eight hours. They had done a route radically harder than ours in a fifth the time. "When did you start?"

"Yesterday at about five."

"At night?"

"Yeah. You want to time it so you're finishing up with some daylight."

I don't remember much more about that exchange, probably because I was so impressed that I more or less stopped speaking for fear of saying something embarrassing. By the next afternoon, however, and by means I have forgotten, I discovered that the man's name was Steve Gerberding, and that he had climbed El Capitan fifty-two times over the last dozen years; fifty-two times on what counts as the climb of a lifetime for a lot of people, a climb so physically demanding as to leave most climbers worn out for weeks. This absolutely fascinated me. I had finally done the thing that was supposed to be the obstacle between me and the rest of my life, and now it appeared that the rest of a life could be devoted to the obstacle itself. Gerberding struck me as a kind of penitent monk who had gone over to the other side, walked up the mountain to pray one day and simply never came back down. I thought of the sailor Bulkington in *Moby Dick*—the one Ishmael sees come ashore after a two-year Pacific whaling cruise only to sign back up for two years' more. El Capitan, I could see, got into your blood and stayed there.

following spread: Gear Selection, Dihedral Wall.

chapter

1

The first words out of the mouth of Royal Robbins, the grand old man of Yosemite climbing, were about how El Capitan has become a kind of lodestone, "because of its plain rock architecture—it's so beautiful in itself, it's so noble, that to have climbed it, to have found your way up it, is to have become more intimate with it and to have become more part of that grandeur, that granite, that *strength* if you will." On a sweaty June day, I'd driven out from San Francisco to meet Robbins, over the Coastal Range and into the humid heat of the Central Valley. Hours away from California's real urban centers, I'd wound among the train yards and warehouses of the agriculture industry, through that sprawling, characterless rural city of broad roads running thick with monstrous SUVs and new American pickups, and eventually found Royal Robbins, Inc., in a small business park shaded by valley oaks. A modestly sized, low-rise building, it had a casual, unpretentious interior layout, with work stations spread around an open floor area and a cheerful receptionist licking envelopes when I walked in. Robbins himself appeared almost immediately—a white-haired man of nearly sixty-five, rigidly upright in his bearing and grave of expression, and wearing cotton pants and a polo shirt bearing his very own version of Ralph Lauren's Polo player: a little hiker, marching forward with straight legs and a long walking stick. Before beginning our talk, Robbins walked me through his operation, showing me a group of women folding wholesome outdoorsy clothes, all in the subdued tones of modesty, integrity, and a certain tidiness of soul. With what seemed to me like feigned pleasure, Robbins also showed me the toy room—a storage space for the employees' white-water kayaks, wetsuits, and related gear, mountain bikes and climbing ropes.

Chuck Pratt, Royal Robbins, and Joe Fitchen, second ascent, the Nose.

Now Robbins and I were sitting at a modest oval conference table surrounded by Robbins's fall ensembles and a library of motivational video tapes for salespeople, and Robbins was free-associating for my benefit, saying that El Capitan has "a certain *manliness*, if you will," and that "if you spend enough time on El Capitan you become more like it."

It occurred to me then that this would be an attractive notion to any young man—this possibility of becoming like a great stone—and that it must have been especially appealing to the boy born Royal Shannon, Jr., in West Virginia in 1935. Truly great mountaineers, by which I mean those who become the defining climbers of an entire era, need a tremendous reservoir of energy, a nearly bottomless competitive aggression, and an insatiable hunger for the next staggering and dangerous achievement. Robbins is unquestionably one such climber, and if we can look for the roots of anyone's ambition in his childhood struggles, then certainly Robbins's youth would seem tailor-made to produce a deep well of rage and a craving for order. In *Royal Robbins, Spirit of the Age*, Pat Ament writes that Robbins's father, after whom Robbins was originally named Royal Shannon, Jr., was a womanizer, minor league baseball player, hunter, and once the state welterweight boxing champion, and that Robbins didn't see him much after the age of three. According to Ament, Robbins's mother, Beulah Robbins, left Shannon at that point and took up with a somewhat violent man named James Chandler. After she married Chandler, he renamed her son James Chandler, Jr., and moved the family to Ohio. A few years later, the boy heard his mother—in the midst of a screaming fight behind a closed door—begging Chandler to please put down the knife. Crawling out a window, the then James Chandler, Jr., called the police. His mother sent him soon after to live with "religious friends" who, as Ament has it, were kind enough to punish the boy's bed-wetting by forcing him to stand under a cold shower with his face to the spray until he nearly drowned. Out in Los Angeles and single again, Beulah told her son to pick a name, and that's when he settled on Royal Robbins—a name that, as Beulah remembers it, gave Robbins a jolt of much-needed self-confidence.

With a working, single mother, little Robbins sold papers, worked as a janitor, washed his own clothes and cooked his own meals, read a lot and kept to himself, and preferred classical music to television. But with all that unsupervised free time, Robbins also started getting in a little trouble, looking for action, riding boxcars out to the Mojave desert and back, and once spending a night in jail on a petty theft charge—he'd stolen some hubcaps with a friend who, when his parents abandoned him to the authorities, spent time in juvenile detention and eventually killed himself. Robbins even took a last trip to Detroit to see his father, perhaps hoping (as would anyone) to fill that empty place in his life. Whatever happened during that visit, and Ament doesn't say, exactly, it made Robbins lose interest in ever seeing Royal Shannon again. By this point, Robbins "was a little confused about everything," Beulah Robbins told Ament, "somewhat traumatized by the events of his life"—at least until, at the age of fifteen, he came upon a book at the library by James Ramsay Ullman. On its jacket cover, Robbins remembers, a climber hung from a steep rock wall, his rope dangling below, and the image struck a chord in the lonely boy. Dangling there in space, the climber looked so calm, so confident, so in control—master of the situation. Inside were such grave bits of wisdom as that "a man is never more a man than when he is striving for what is beyond his grasp," and that "there is no conquest worth the winning save that over [our] own weakness and ignorance and fear." Ullman's other great climbing book, *Banner in the Sky*, which is still in

following spread: Royal Robbins at the El Cap Tower bivouac, first ascent, the Salathé Wall.

print and with exactly the cover Robbins described for *High Conquest*, would have spoken to Robbins even more. A rousing novel for young adults, *Banner in the Sky* tells of a sixteen-year-old Swiss boy attempting to conquer the great mountain on which his father died, despite his lonely mother's wish that he settle down and become a hotel manager. Along the dangerous way to the summit, the fatherless boy saves another climber from death, wins the respect and adoration of his entire village, and finds out what it means to be a man. But whichever Ullman title Robbins read, Robbins describes his discovery of Ullman as a kind of eureka moment, admitting that he saw his whole future in the simple image on that book jacket—deciding that he would become precisely the climber depicted and that he would give his life to the mountains. Seeing climbing, in other words, as a means of fashioning a stronger, more confident self. In short order, Robbins and a few friends were hitchhiking to Yosemite, ropes in hand.

Unskilled fifteen-year-olds can't really get off the ground in the Valley, so Robbins soon retreated to Southern California, enrolled in a Sierra Club climbing class, and then dropped out of high school to work at a ski area in the San Gabriel Mountains. While finishing high school at night, however, and climbing at small Southern California crags like Tahquitz Rock, Robbins acquired a local reputation and met several other young climbers— including a championship sailor and future Stanford engineering graduate named Tom Frost, eventual Patagonia founder Yvon Chouinard, the famous funnyman T. M. Herbert, and Warren Harding, all of them now legendary in climbing circles. Soon enough, Robbins was making a name for himself in Yosemite—though not, at first, on El Capitan.

"In the early days," Robbins told me, "you noticed El Cap, but we didn't pay much attention to it, because it was kind of quote-unquote out of the question. We didn't even consider climbing it—it was too much of an imaginative leap. You might say, 'Well, you take enough time, you're going to get to the top,' but even that wasn't known for sure. We didn't have enough experience on three-thousand-foot rock walls to know what would happen to you, what would happen to your mind and so forth, after so many days on it. It was just a big blank space like the middle of Africa was at one time. You might say, Well, if we go to the middle of Africa, we might find a river, might find crocodiles, might find warriors, whatever, or you might find almost anything. You don't know if you can get there, you don't know what's going to happen to you before you really actually try, and that was the way with El Cap. It was just a big unknown. It wasn't that we had specific things we weren't sure of. Those existed too, but it was just so big. It was so much bigger than anything that had been done that we didn't seriously let it enter our minds and so we weren't obsessed with it as a climbing thing until after it had been climbed."

Thus, in 1955, Robbins's fixation with the also-unclimbed two-thousand-foot northwest face of Half Dome. According to the Yosemite climbing historian Steve Roper, a team of older climbers had taken a crack at it in 1954, only to turn back after 175 feet. The following year, Robbins, Warren Harding, and two others spent three days struggling only a few hundred feet higher. For the next couple of years, Robbins plotted, picking out a likely route for the upper part of the wall and hand-forging chrome-molybdenum pitons to drive into the big cracks above. Then, in 1957, Robbins and two partners spent five days meandering across that vertical wilderness, banging pitons into the rock, sleeping at night in nylon flight suit coveralls, living on a quart of water each per day and a diet of tuna, raisins, nuts, dates, and the like. In order to communicate with their friends' on the ground, they worked out a flashlight signalling code to be practiced only during the Valley's evening "Firefall" event—thus reducing the chance that any sensation would be made of their climb. It's hard to imagine the drive and courage this must have required, given that Half Dome dwarfed the achievements of the older, established generation of Yosemite climbers. Embarking more or less into the unknown, on a face that gets considerably worse weather and lower temperatures than the rest of the Valley, the twenty-one-year-old Robbins had quite literally pulled off the greatest rock climb ever done on American soil.

Robbins, along with friends like Tom Frost and Yvon Chouinard, also seems to have begun developing, at about this time, the peculiar code of climbing behavior that so defines his presence in climbing history. Frost and Chouinard—very different men, and every bit as compelling and influential as Robbins—have both spoken of climbing, at one time or another, as a kind of spiritual path. At the very center of Robbins's character one senses something slightly different: a craving for a coherent way of being in the world, an orderly philosophy and ethic of his own design, a means to self-improvement and self-mastery. Indeed, Robbins's greatest contribution to climbing may well be the articulation he eventually gave to this impulse, and the way it came to define the core values of mountaineering, combining James Ramsay Ullman's ideas about conquering your fears with Ralph Waldo Emerson's deeply American belief that the golden age is always at hand. Robbins had also picked up a strict environmentalism from John Salathé, the greatest Yosemite climber of the generation preceding Robbins's, as well as a belief from British poet Geoffrey Winthrop Young, that "It's not getting to the top that counts, it's the way you do it." Climbing mountains, in other words, is a meaningless business for its own sake, and only becomes a grand undertaking when practiced within certain parameters that maintain risk, challenge, and uncertainty—rules that safeguard, in other words, the element of adventure.

Robbins's generation turned all of this homespun American wisdom into a system of climbing ethics, with minimalism, respect for the rock, and boldness as paramount virtues. In effect, this meant (and still means) that the greatest—and therefore both the most admirable and the most personally satisfying—climb will be the one using a minimum of gear, climbers, and time, and ideally taking a single, self-contained push up the steepest, most direct route to the summit. It will also be the one that does as little damage to the wall as possible, and avoids anything that reduces uncertainty, like preliminary reconnaissance, fixed lines providing an easy escape to the ground, excessive supplies, and, most of all, an excessive reliance on technology, particularly in the form of permanent drilled anchors. Though admittedly not conscious of it in the moment, Robbins and other likeminded climbers of the period will say now that they were following an unspoken, unwritten principle: doing things the hard way makes you a better, stronger person; taking the easy way does just the opposite. These men were also very much creating the climbing world that the rest of us—as alpinists, I mean—live in every day.

• • •

The *American Heritage Dictionary* defines a "golden age" as "a period of great peace, prosperity, and happiness," deriving from the term's use in Greek and Roman mythology as "the first age of the world, an untroubled and prosperous era during which people lived in ideal happiness." When used in reference to a sport like climbing, the emphasis is on "first age of the world," the period when a sport flowers into a coherent culture, when its practice and techniques are at last up to the great challenges, and the great challenges are still available for the taking. If Yosemite climbing can be said to have had such a golden age, then it began with Royal Robbins's first ascent of Half Dome in 1957, ended with Robbins's final statement on El Capitan in 1970, and was defined in large part by the differences between Robbins and the man who actually climbed El Capitan first.

Born eleven years before Robbins, in 1924, Warren Harding grew up dirt poor in mountain California during the Depression. When the Second World War came around, he was turned down for military service on account of a heart murmur—something that, Harding told me when I drove over to visit him at an RV park in the eastern Sierra, hurt his feelings pretty bad. That is, until he started seeing "all those big, healthy, jocky-type guys coming home with their asses blown completely off." Harding spent the duration as an airplane propellor mechanic in Sacramento, fixing war-damaged p-38s from the Pacific theatre, and found himself unemployed at age twenty-two after the armistice. Driving around Sacramento one day, he saw a guy holding a stick upright for a surveying party and thought, "Hey, there's something I could probably do." Landing work for the State of California Department of Highways, Harding was a self-supporting adult with his own place to live when he finally took up climbing at twenty-eight, the age when most people are quitting the sport. (Climbing was also the only thing he'd ever been good at, Harding later joked to a reporter: "I couldn't catch a ball or any of that stuff. I could only do what required brute stupidity.")

Temperamentally, Harding couldn't have been more different from Robbins—a clown-contrarian rather than a philosopher, a hard-drinking and irreverent man with zero interest in any code of ethics. Referring to Robbins's earnest group of proselytizers by his favorite old epithet for them, "the Valley Christians," Harding told me that he never understood the big words they all used, and he suspected that they did vocabulary building exercises just to show off. For example, Harding explained, over a glass of wine, "When Roper said things like, 'We were young and full of hubris,' I always misunderstood him. I didn't know what 'hubris' was, and from the context I took it to mean a brownish, foul-smelling stuff much like what comes out of horse's assholes." Later on, after he was famous, Harding even published a climbing manifesto of his own, a book called *Downward Bound, A Mad Guide to Rock-Climbing*, announcing the Lower Sierra Eating, Drinking, and Farcing Society, founded because the Sierra Club and American Alpine Club appeal to those of more lofty values. The book celebrated the baser characteristics of alpinists, like "drunkenness, gluttony, sloth, cowardice, treachery, lechery," and offered warnings about the risks of climbing drunk alongside observations (and illustrations) about the pleasure of watching girls climb from directly below. One drawing, rendered by Harding's then-girlfriend, depicted Harding as a naked, winged Satan.

Having returned to Yosemite Valley to try the first ascent of Half Dome with his own team, Harding was surprised to find Robbins already topping out. All dressed up with nowhere to go, Harding, Mark Powell, and Dolt Feuerer went straight to work on the greatest Yosemite plum of all, the first ascent of El Capitan. For two full seasons, they climbed in precisely the style Robbins deplored, sieging the wall in classic Himalayan fashion—fixing lines from the ground to their slowly advancing high point, running supplies up and down, retreating for long breaks on the ground and then ascending again and again.

Harding "went through partners on this extended ordeal," in the ungenerous words of Robbins, "like Elizabeth Taylor through husbands," and experimented with a variety of novel gear, like pitons forged from the legs of old stoves and a bicycle-wheeled cart for dragging supplies up the smooth face.

Because of the huge tourist crowds Harding's climb drew—and the traffic jams caused by those crowds—the Park Service put El Cap off-limits to Harding for the entire summer of 1958, and then gave him an autumn ultimatum: finish by Thanksgiving, or give it up altogether. On November 12, 1958, after forty-five days of siege climbing, a hundred and twenty-five drilled expansion bolts, countless hammered pitons and hauled gear bags, Harding embarked on a final eleven-day summit push. For the last seventeen straight hours, the hard-hat highway worker hand-drilled twenty-eight consecutive bolts, right through the night, and put the party over the top at dawn. As he stumbled away from the rim and into an enormous crowd of well-wishers, Harding later wrote, "it was not at all clear to me who was conqueror and who was conquered: I do recall that El Cap was in much better condition than I was." Irrespective of who won the fight, the climb changed Harding's life: a gaggle of reporters awaited him on top, and he was forever after the first man to climb El Capitan.

• • •

Although most mountaineers will insist that they practice their sport for strictly personal reasons, climbing is a deeply competitive activity, torn, like so much of what we do, between the desire to live only for oneself, independent of the opinions of others, and the craving for recognition. Everything about

Harding's approach to climbing the Nose threatened the terms by which Robbins lived, treating the wall like a vast, absurdist engineering project instead of a fortifying quest. If you commit yourself as deeply to a sport as Robbins had to climbing, and base your very sense of self-worth on your achievements within it, then the rules defining those achievements can only acquire enormous significance. Indeed, one can read Robbins's subsequent decade of climbing and writing as a sustained and very successful campaign to reassert the primacy of his own way: Robbins joined, for example, the great free-climber Chuck Pratt, early aid-climbing wizard Frost, and Joe Fitschen on the second ascent of the Nose, repeating Harding's route in a single one-week push, without fixed ropes, and declaring the achievement "an important first ascent in its own right." (Which it simply was not; it was a historically important second ascent. Robbins himself has since made this point in print.) Robbins also made the second ascent of Harding's route on the east face of Washington Column, again with Frost, and he announced afterwards that they had halved Harding's climbing time and even chopped bolts deemed unnecessary to the climb.

For his next act, Robbins teamed up with Frost and Pratt in picking out an entirely new line on the southwest face of El Cap, to be called the Salathé Wall, in honor of their great mentor. In the aftermath of this truly extraordinary outing, Robbins offered a precise accounting of their use of ropes and bolts, and of the coherence of their team. It should be said that this was still a game without clear rules, and that by declaring such statistics Robbins was helping to author the modern sport of rock-climbing; by their shared commitment to an ideal, he and Frost and Pratt were creating a path meant not to be traveled once, for strictly personal glory, but to offer a valid and adventurous way to achievement for all subsequent climbers, for time immemorial. Precisely because of its limited use of bolts and ropes and supporting climbers, the Salathé was a very real gift to every climbing generation to follow. Robbins was also, however, engaging in the timeless mountaineering tradition of one-upsmanship, enumerating all the ways in which his climb was superior to Harding's Nose effort. When a third new route went up on El Cap, Ed Cooper's 1962 Dihedral Wall climb, Robbins helped Frost knock off the second ascent in far shorter time, and then publicly criticized the siege style (or "easy way" nature) of the first ascent. Likewise with Harding's route on the Leaning Tower: Robbins not only repeated the route completely alone and in a storm—the first American solo of a big wall—but, once again, in better time. In need of a rest, and wanted back home at work, Galen Rowell and Ed Cooper left fixed lines on a new route on Half Dome, a route that threatened to diminish the pre-eminence of Robbins's original route, and Robbins grabbed Dick McCracken, ascended their lines, and stole the first ascent on the premise that the others were sieging it in improper style. ("I saw that I could kind of own Half Dome," Robbins told me in another context, adding that "it would make a great tombstone.")

The first ascent of North America Wall, on the southeast face of El Cap, done by the dream team of Chouinard, Frost, Pratt, and Robbins, in 1963, was the hardest technical route in the world at the time, and afterwards Robbins publicly declared that "The era of siege climbing via fixed ropes is past," as if the world were still comparing him unfavorably to Harding and Cooper. Robbins even admitted later, with admirable (and characteristic) self-awareness, that his competitive ambition had gone so far by that point that, "I was getting greedy. I was anxious to get a certain wall before someone else did, and a new route on El Capitan would be that much more to add to one's reputation.

So I started thinking more in terms of doing climbs for fame than of doing them just for the fun of it." When Yvon Chouinard and T. M. Herbert did the first ascent of their Muir Wall route on El Capitan in even better style than North America Wall—with only two climbers, zero reconnaissance, and a minimum of gear—Robbins promptly soloed the second ascent. As he put it, this was the only way he could think of to do something scarier still. Steve Roper even recalls Robbins's suggesting a forthcoming guidebook include "first continuous" ascents along with first ascent listings, a move that would have assured Robbins's primacy even on routes he had not personally established.

But a decade's journey on the very cutting edge of big wall climbing should never be reduced to the pettiness of competition, the least part of its whole. This must have been a truly miraculous time for all of these men, the immediate world very much their oyster and tremendous, historic, and very worthwhile achievements perfectly available, the country prospering and the camping cheap. The first ascent of the Salathé Wall, regardless of its relationship to Harding's Nose route, was an adventure of unparalleled majesty, with Frost, Pratt, and Robbins hammering their way up a truly unknown face for fully a week, with no lifeline to the ground, no idea what they would find, and no rescue remotely possible—a trio of friends adrift on a sea of granite, navigating by cracks, dihedrals, and overhangs. By fixing ropes only on the climb's first third, and then casting off even those escape lines when they began their summit push, they set a new standard for commitment—as if even the experience of climbing a new route on an untouched wall of El Capitan would benefit from the tweaking of conditions.

The climb wandered across elusive slabs, through a pendulum swing to a relentless and unprotectable off-width that still puts strong climbers into fits of apopleptic fear, and then up to the ghastly "Ear" off-width, a massive chunk of rock that hangs off the wall like a gargantuan earlobe. Whole hours were lost in trying to bypass this "frightening formation," as Robbins called it, a Bombay door-style chimney that eventually required thirty feet of horizontal shimmying, back against the wall proper, feet against the inside wall of that overhanging earlobe, and the abyss yawning miserably beneath— "Tom [Frost] led this anxiety-producing pitch," Robbins dryly recalled, "with nearly perfect composure . . . only a few screams of terror and moans of horror." Frost himself, a wonderfully dignified, generous, and good-spirited man, told me recently that they were not just the only rock climbers on El Capitan that week, but in all of Yosemite Valley, and that only their girlfriends knew they were even up there. Exploring and creating simultaneously, Frost, Pratt, and Robbins established what is still considered the greatest pure rock climb in the world, legendary nearly forty years later not because anyone bested Harding (all will agree readily that the Nose is a masterpiece in its own right) but because the Salathé Wall has such integrity, expressing so perfectly the positive ideals by which it was climbed.

North America Wall required more commitment still, given its over-hanging and wandering nature—rendering it most probably irreversible. Chouinard, in fact, figures there was only one other climber in the United States capable of rescuing them—Layton Kor, who was then in Colorado. Having scouted only the first third of the route, the team started up this time without a single fixed line, and on climbing of extremely high difficulty— with Frost falling when a horn of rock broke on the second pitch, and Chouinard blowing out a piece of gear on the third. One long blank section was crossed by lowering Frost sixty feet off of a bolt above, until he was hanging thirty feet straight across from the rest of the party—who then hauled Frost in and let him go, such that he flew sideways to a distant flake. Some of the terrain was so overhung that following team members, who ascended lines secured above, swung out as much as fifty feet before prusiking straight upwards. On the morning of the seventh day, while the team ate a salami and cheese breakfast in what they called the "Black Cave," Robbins's wife, Liz, radioed news of an approaching storm. Pratt got right to work hammering his way out of the overhung ceiling of this cave, on a lead Robbins declared the most spectacular in American climbing, and just after the rain hit they made it to the base of the "Cyclops Eye," a two-hundred-foot-high shallow cavern near the top of El Capitan, where they found relative shelter. The next morning, during a brief break in what was forecast to be a three-day storm, Chouinard pounded upwards by way of large pitons driven directly between loose, overhanging blocks, and Robbins finally placed the team's thirty-eighth and last bolt, still a full three hundred feet from the valley rim. The next day, after nine consecutive days on a devious, wandering line, the group "shook hands on top, as happy as pagans." They had pioneered El Capitan's steepest, smoothest face (now known colloquially and absurdly as "the man's side of the stone,") and established what was at the time the single hardest rock climb ever done.

The "big four," as *Mountain* magazine editor Ken Wilson has called them, "Robbins, Pratt, Frost, and Chouinard together seemed to exert a very strong moral force, Pratt silent and brilliant, Frost cheerful, humble, and friendly, yet with that religious dignity, Chouinard impish, quite sharp and critical yet skillful, a great trend-setter, and Robbins an almost Buddha-like presence, a supreme dignity tinged with courage to say and do controversial

following spread: Warren Harding's mother looking at Warren Harding's then companion, herself looking up at Warren Harding, during the first ascent of Wall of the Early Morning Light, 1970.

things, a sort of moral leadership in both words as well as deeds." Pratt, in the words of Robbins, "like Jack London and Thomas Wolfe . . . is an incorrigible romantic and suffers from the anguish which is a corollary of that *Weltanschauung*. Perhaps Chuck loves climbing partly because rock walls, unlike humans, are without malice." Of Chouinard, Robbins wrote that "If there was ever anyone who has an eye for elegant routes on esthetic walls, it is he. A poetic soul, Chouinard really rather disdains the analytical mind, for he hates to see beautiful things ripped and torn. He has the kind of mind which would make a good artist, but a poor chess player. Maddeningly creative, Chouinard has invented more techniques and devices in climbing than anyone I know." Together, these men were creating not just the modern culture of rock-climbing, but to some degree contemporary outdoors California. While hand-forging gear to sell from the back of his car in Yosemite, Chouinard had single-handedly reinvented the rock-climbing gear used everywhere in the world—he once claimed, with complete justification, that not a single major ascent had been made in North America after 1958 without the use of his equipment. With the help of Frost's gift for applied engineering, Chouinard made a similar impact on alpine climbing gear—as these two produced the world's first rigid crampons. In fact, in later years, Chouinard's equipment company had lesser but still notable effects on the blossoming sports of backcountry skiing and white-water kayaking, more or less created the genre of clothing we now consider technical outdoor wear, and Chouinard is currently at work reinventing the surfboard. (Frost, for his part, helped invent and found a company to produce what are now the gold standard of soft photographic lighting boxes.) And despite all this, T. M. Herbert recalls that Chouinard only worked two months a year. "The rest of the time he'd be off climbing. He'd clean some old woman's garage once in a while to get a few dollars, but that was about it. He'd buy old second-hand gear, and wear old shoes stuffed with paper in them because they were too big. That's the way he lived! He just existed! We thought he'd either starve to death or be a hobo for the rest of his life." According to Frost, "Half the time he'd go down to the beach, throw his anvil down on the sand, and make pitons until the waves got good enough to surf."

Though Robbins's accounts of his great climbs with these men are marred by assertions of superiority to earlier climbs, they also sing with elation at the experience itself, of snow dusting the valley rim after climbing the Salathé, and of "feeling very spiritually rich indeed" as the team descended after their victory. Likewise, the memories of his compadres: Picking out the Salathé route from the meadow below, Frost told me, his kind pale eyes filled with clear-sighted wonder, "was like being Huckleberry Finn, just starting down the river." Chouinard's description of his first ascent of the John Muir Wall—which, like the Salathé, is named in humble homage, not self-aggrandizement—is truly a classic of climbing literature, laying out yet again the Valley climber's strict minimalist ethic and describing his and T. M. Herbert's absolute commitment to it. Chouinard puts the basis for their lightweight approach—minimal water, food, and equipment—in John Muir's own minimalist ramblings and fastings in the Sierra, and in John Salathé and Axe Nelson's long journey on the 1947 first ascent of the Lost Arrow Chimney, even in the nine-day ascent of the North America Wall and its discoveries "about the constant adaptation of the body to the conditions, to harder work, less food, less water." Chouinard positions the Muir Wall climb as only the obvious next step in this nameless path: "another first ascent on 'El Cap' in one push with two men instead of four." Calculating supplies down to the "last piton and last cup of water," they climbed well for three days before a downpour began; by the next, temperatures had dropped, and soon Chouinard is quoting Herzog on Annapurna, to the effect that, "The cost of a failure can be dear, but the values to be gained from a success can be so marvelous as often to change a person's whole life." These values include, as the climb and the rain wore on and food and water wore out, a vision of a peregrine falcon eyrie deep in a chimney; "soft white pieces of down stuck on to the crystals of grey granite."

Eventually, Chouinard comes to feel utterly at home on the wall, looking 2500 feet down and recognizing it all as another life, and he begins to see the world anew, losing himself in the individual crystals in the granite, the varied shapes of the clouds, tiny bugs scampering about the walls. Think of it as very real spiritual ecstasy, reminding T. M. of childhood days on the family porch, under the setting sun, and leaving Chouinard with the feeling that, while the wall itself has not changed, he personally has absorbed some of its "strength and serenity." In an article called "The Climber as Visionary" (Ascent, 1969), Doug Robinson sees Chouinard's visions as the direct result of the suffering produced by his purist climbing ethic: "It is a system," Robinson writes. "You need only copy the ingredients and commit yourself to them. They lead to the door. It is not necessary to attain to Chouinard's technical level—few can or do—only to his degree of commitment."

It appears that doing things the hard way is a double-edged impulse, offering the undeniable attraction of demonstrating to the world that you can do things the hard way, but also giving the sport of mountaineering the only meaning it has.

· · ·

Warren Harding stayed off El Capitan for thirteen years after his first ascent of the Nose, a period in which Robbins was extremely active, and in which his anti-siege, anti-bolting ethics had become the law of the Valley's little domain. A vibrant subculture had sprouted in Camp 4, the Yosemite climbers' campground, as climbers from all over the country crowded into that squalid tent-city, and yet Frost, for one, doesn't remember seeing Harding much, only that Harding was somehow watching whenever they repeated one of his routes. As Frost has it—in a characteristically fond memory—Harding would usually say something friendly and gracious to the effect of, "You guys are amazing, you know that? You're way better climbers than me." Then, in 1970, the now forty-six-year-old Harding "met a rather unsavory character, name of Dean 'Wizard' Caldwell," with whom he shared many qualities, including the fact that "we were both rather lazy . . . an important quality of the serious climber. We talked much of past glories and future plans. But for the most part didn't actually do anything."

Eventually, while "completely taken by Demon Rum, we decided we would climb El Capitan's Wall of the Early Morning Light . . . the Big Motha' Climb!" The Valley's finest climbers, including the hot young Jim Bridwell, had been exploring this line for some time—an exquisitely steep and smooth sweep of pale stone between the Nose and North America Wall, perhaps the most imposing part of the entire massif—but they had all backed off because of their reluctance to bolt the long blank sections. That fall, with a healthy supply-sponsorship from Christian Brothers winery, Harding and Caldwell began ferrying loads to the base, with a "cloak of secrecy surrounding our

following spread: Yvon Chouinard, first ascent, North America Wall.

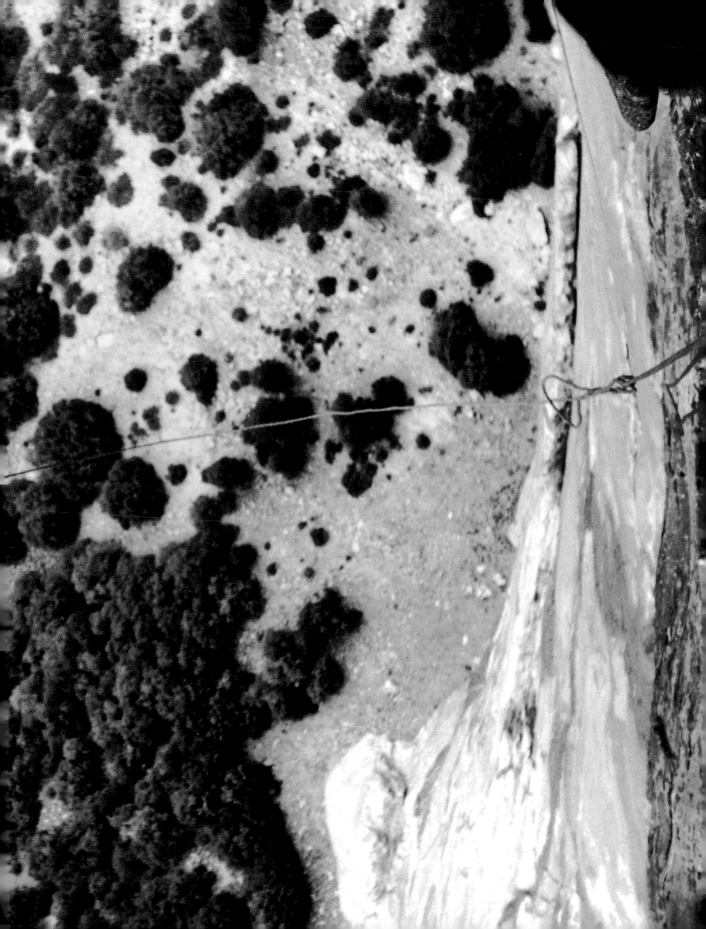

activities" because of the "great hairy giants all around waiting to annihilate any trespassers on 'their route.'"

While waiting out bad weather at a friend's house, "we were shocked to learn that the dreaded Royal Robbins had suddenly appeared in the valley . . . what now? Would he come charging up the wall . . . just plow us under? Desperately, we moved out." The climb began somewhat inauspiciously, with an advertising photo shoot for Christian Brothers, in which Harding sipped wine from a crystal glass while swinging through space, and with a furious explosion of rage from Caldwell, rumored to be related to the need for a mood-stabilizing injection. ("Oh, shit," Harding thought, "what have I gotten myself into?") Their progress was slowed from the start by Harding's having a bad knee, the result of an unfortunate encounter with a fast-moving truck. Then a powerful storm set the team back, as did a violent shitting and pecking attack when Caldwell disturbed a bird's nest on a high ledge. Stretching two weeks' water and food for an unprecedented single push of twenty-seven days, without fixed ropes, and drilling a total of 330 holes, Harding and Caldwell's climb of the Wall of the Early Morning Light (also known as the Dawn Wall) received the most media attention ever lavished on an American mountaineering achievement. The spark that ignited it came on the twentieth day of the climb, when a rescue effort was organized, assuming the climbers were out of water and incapacitated, so slowly were they moving. Ropes were already being lowered off the edge of the wall when Harding noticed some-one walking around at the base of the route. Calling down, he was surprised to find that it was T. M. Herbert, and more surprised still to discover that Herbert had come to save the climbers. Declining politely, Harding imagined later some "rather bizarre scenes: rescuers landing on Timothy Tower [named

Warren Harding.

for the main Christian Brother] to find the 'exhausted' climbing team enjoying a fine mini-feast of salami, cheese, bread, and an entire bottle of Cabernet Sauvignon (Christian Brothers, of course) all in a beautiful moon-lit setting. Dialogue: 'Good evening! What can we do for you?'

'We've come to rescue you.'

'Really? Come now, get hold of yourselves—have some wine . . .' maybe the rescuers quietly going home in the morning, or maybe a piton hammer fight as they tried to take the climbers with them."

Harding topped out to a crowd of well-wishers and reporters offering bottles of champagne and piles of food, and he remembers falling apart in tears at the sight, clutching his girlfriend while Caldwell hugged a local woman of whom he'd grown fond (much to the dismay of his Oregon girlfriend and the woman's boyfriend, both of whom were watching the scene on television). Harding's mother was even there, put up for free at the Yosemite Lodge along with Caldwell's godparents, and if Harding had been Mr. El Cap after the Nose, well, now he was the toast of the national media, covered by the "Wide World of Sports," interviewed on the "Merv Griffin Show," and profiled in magazines. Harding and Caldwell were quickly flown to New York City and then on to Hollywood and San Francisco for various television shows. The climb certainly merited as much attention as any, but Harding himself would have admitted that this newfound "famiosity," as he called it, had less to do with the climb's difficulty than with its performance art qualities: the ludicrous amount of time spent in what seemed like an odd form of flagpole sitting, the demonstration of a perverse kind of perseverance to no meaningful end (Harding once cracked that climbing was all about finding the hardest ways of getting nowhere). If Robbins was the esoteric superhero setting extreme examples for the initiated few, Harding was everyman, with all his limitations and maybe a loose screw or two.

Harding wrote later that if he could have foreseen what would happen over the next few months, maybe he would have jumped off the cliff the moment he topped out. In the middle of the following winter, Harding and Caldwell were giving a slide presentation at a National Sport Show in Chicago when they heard that Robbins and a man named Don Lauria had started up their route with a chisel, and were chopping all of Harding's bolts, removing what they thought was "a blot on the Yosemite landscape." After four pitches of chopping, Robbins did lose faith and stop, eventually summiting after six uneventful days of climbing, but the muddled and bitter damage was done. (Harding quipped in horror that Robbins had become a kind of Alpine Carry Nation, likening him to the hatchet-wielding temperance activist who once described herself as "a bulldog running along at the feet of Jesus, barking at what He doesn't like," and who became famous in the early part of the century for storming into bars screaming "Smash, ladies! Smash!" and hacking furniture to pieces, all in the hopes of outlawing alcoholic beverages.) For all its banality and mean bitterness, and despite the fact that both Robbins and Harding see it as absurdly overblown in significance, the Dawn Wall episode has become one of the great foundational legends of Yosemite climbing, filled with import—the moment when the Titans clashed. If we can indulge in a fantasy of the 1960s as a time of innocence in Yosemite climbing, then certainly this was its Fall, when both Harding and Robbins made the most voluble statements of their climbing careers and both came away diminished.

I met Harding beside an aspen-shaded creek, at a vintage Airstream owned by old friends of his, Roger Derryberry and Mary Lou Long. At seventy-five, Harding wore velcro-strap sneakers and an oversized t-shirt with a picture of El Cap looming above a little handicap access sign. He still had the Satanic visage, though a little plumped, mellowed, and crazed by time, no longer a devilishly handsome James Dean so much as an unrepentant old demon. Over dinner, in the warm light of an East Side summer dusk, Harding reiterated a line I'd read in Galen Rowell's *The Vertical World of Yosemite*, that Harding had only climbed the Dawn Wall because he liked the way it looked and didn't care how many bolts it took, and that he never set out to "build highways," and didn't "give a rat's ass what Royal did with the route, or what he thought he accomplished." Sipping Chardonnay, Harding dismissed even that response now, recounting how he fell out of his seat laughing when Lauria, Robbins's accomplice, apologized for the whole thing. It was nice to believe that Harding could take all this so lightly; the first ascent of the Nose and the first ascent of the Dawn Wall were the only two times Harding ever climbed El Capitan in the old days, and in the years afterwards, while he'd continued to work as a highway and construction surveyor, he'd been on the lecture circuit for quite a while, offering his bawdy and off-beat "Downward Bound" slide show at climbing stores, film festivals, and colleges around the country. He still does the show, in fact—still plays Mr. El Capitan once in a while—and why not? The triumphs of youth ought to carry us through with some kind of equanimity.

I knew, however, that on Harding's last Yosemite first ascent, on the Porcelain Wall in 1978, he'd told his partner to chop every single bolt they placed, after they'd moved above it, as if in a conscious act of self-mutilation. ("Because I'm a nasty asshole," Harding replied now, when I asked why he'd done this.) I learned also that Harding's last time on El Cap (in his days as an active climber) was for a film-reenactment of the Nose climb, scheduled for shooting by Derryberry in 1978. Another climber apparently had to be hired to do all the leading because, as Harding's friend Mary Lou said, partly in jest, while fixing Harding some dessert, "Warren was drinking too much by that time," and had also scheduled one too many female companions for the adventure. When three very irritated women showed up, the unpleasant scene seems to have been the final straw on a pile of logistical snags that broke the project. ("I've always had a terrible time with women," Harding admitted ruefully.) And despite the humor of *Downward Bound*, an enormous amount of the book's energy is devoted to defending against imaginary persecutions, ridiculing fictional accusers. It even includes a rather long, involved appendix, a kind of get-even scorecard, listing every notable climber of the era and giving Harding's judgment on their character. (Albeit in characteristically inverted terms, with his own status as the lowest of the low, and Yvon Chouinard, "the gymnosophist climber . . . even more spiritual and certainly cleaner than Royal Robbins but [lacking] the overall pizzazz to be God. Will have to settle for sainthood.") In fact, when I pressed, asking if he hadn't been rankled by all the bolt counting in Steve Roper's *Camp 4*, the definitive history of those years, Harding growled, "I'd love to kick Roper's fucking ass. I'm not kidding. If I bump into him some day, one of us is going to get hurt, and it won't be me." Clearly, Harding cared.

Royal Robbins, Inc., of course, is a very different place for a man to pass his time; where Harding made a cottage industry out of self-effacement, Robbins made a very real one out of self-respect. As with Harding, I had asked Robbins just to talk about El Cap at first, and he'd done so graciously— first with those remarks about the "strength" of El Capitan, and how it rubs off on you, and also recounting his various climbs, the beauty of the wall, the pleasure of good companionship. Robbins gives corporate motivational speeches based on his climbing philosophy, and if they are anything like the slide show I saw him give, they use tales of his adventures as parables, demonstrating the importance of self-reliance, team work, healthy competition, and the life-long benefits to be gained from doing things the hard way. His rap, needless to say, is pretty well honed, and I didn't get any real sense of the man until I brought up the Dawn Wall bolt-chopping episode, near the end of our talk. Like Harding, Robbins was dismissive at first, calling it all pure silliness. But then I asked about the time he went up on El Capitan after the Wall of the Early Morning Light, intending to solo a new route to the right of North America Wall. The climbing on that part of El Capitan is, for the most part, harder than on either Wall of the Early Morning Light or North America Wall, and nobody had ever even tried to solo a new El Cap route. In one stroke, Robbins would have both forever one-upped Harding's last route and erased the embarassment of his chopping episode. Robbins also would have taken a step into the future with that climb, pioneering a swath of El Cap that fell, as it happened, to the next generation—Jim Dunn, only a year later. In the end, Robbins got about a third of the way up, decided he didn't have enough bolts to finish the job, and came down.

The old hunger, as Robbins put it, had begun to leave him by that point, and fair enough. Life does have its seasons, after all. But when I asked now if there was any relationship between the Dawn Wall fiasco and the attempt on that last route, Robbins said firmly and quickly that there was not, that it was just the natural next step. He sounded vaguely angry when I asked if he'd done any El Cap routes after that one, and he said that he had

Tom Frost, first ascent, the Salathé Roof.

not, as far as he could remember. I knew already that in the years following, while a young climber named Jim Bridwell took over Yosemite and arthritis made climbing impossible for Robbins, Robbins took up kayaking and soon scored important first descents of three major rivers in California and several in Chile. I knew also that after a quickly aborted first marriage (to a woman he met in Vegas while he was still virtually a kid, and who, as it turned out, was already married and a mother) Robbins had been lucky enough to find the love of his life, a very beautiful, well bred, and educated young woman from San Francisco who was working as a hostess at Yosemite's posh Ahwahnee Hotel. Together they'd raised a good family and created the successful clothing business that now consumed most of their time. It has been a remarkable life, and if anyone ever decides to judge Robbins by the measure of his sustained passion—and it won't be a bad idea—he will have very few peers. So I was surprised by what he said next.

In the old days, the young Robbins had agonized at length about the mysterious nature of his climbing ambition, seeing it alternately as a search for oneself and for the courage to face what he saw as humankind's galling insignificance in the universe and what he called "the chilling spectre of inevitable death." ("Some people are bothered by thoughts of decay and death," Robbins wrote elsewhere. "Not me. Rather, I am obsessed. Death . . . decay . . . decay and death.") In an account of climbing the west face of El Cap with T. M. Herbert, Robbins called climbing "a game in which we play at acquiring the courage necessary to a beautiful life." In another mood, he once described all of his life's ongoing struggles as an attempt to find peace of mind in some hypothetical ultimate climb that would make everything else all right. Self-knowledge is not, however, synonymous with liberation from the self, and where Harding could find solace in the absurdity of what he'd done with his life, Robbins seemed always to want it all to add up. On one wall of his company's office, I'd seen a chart mapping sales projections over a drawing of El Cap, with gradually ascending figures tacked to each of the original bivouac points on the Salathé Wall route, hundreds of thousands of dollars in the Free Blast and millions on the Headwall above; he'd mentioned that the real adventure of his life these days was in trying to build a company "with some of the qualities of the climbs I did." Perhaps he was just thinking of Yvon Chouinard, who truly has built such a company—Patagonia, somehow exploding with success even as Chouinard insists on playing by his old rules, strictly limiting his advertising, sending catalogues only to those who request them, using all organic cotton and devoting a real percentage of proceeds to environmental causes. And even if Robbins wasn't thinking of Chouinard, America just does this to us—it whittles away at our non-remunerative achievements, declares again and again that only dollars count. So it's natural that Robbins would still be trying, even thirty years later, to translate that dazzling early success into an affluent adulthood.

Nevertheless, thinking now of that final, aborted route, Robbins wrung his gnarled hands with a surprising passion, and he focused his riveting eyes on a point somewhere in the vacant sheen of the table. Sixty-four years old and incontrovertibly sanctified as one of this nation's truly great climbers, Robbins pressed his lips together as if the painful memory of this one, inconsequential failure overrode all his successes, as if perhaps *that* had been the one, ultimate climb that would have made everything all right. I don't know Robbins in any real way, so I can't know how true this impression was—doubtless his family and business weigh powerfully on his mind, along with the other private demons we all carry around. But I thought of what he'd said at the very beginning of our interview, how El Capitan was a kind of lodestone, so noble that climbing it brought you closer to its "manliness," so that you became more like it; I thought also of his reading James Ramsay Ullman, taking so seriously, at that formative moment in his life, the idea that we seek not to conquer the mountain, but to conquer ourselves.

"You know," he said now, "if I had held on with that route, I probably could have done it, because it turned out that there were cracks up above and there weren't any, you know, blank walls. I probably did have enough bolts. And it would have been more honorable to have pushed it higher too. I didn't . . . and I'm a little ashamed of that, frankly. It was a moment of weakness."

An astonishing remark, I thought, as if somehow he could have been—should still become!—like the rock that is El Cap.

following spread: Yvon Chouinard and Royal Robbins hunkered down in
a storm, first ascent, North America Wall.

chapter

2

Maybe it's the thick, warped shape of his fingers—
claw-like forms that grip yours
with an odd kind of passivity, as if this spring-loaded steel trap just can't bring itself to engage for anything short of a hammer. Maybe it's the feeling you get of rude, somehow skeletal, strength-in-age, like that of men who've done hard physical work all their lives—the square shoulders, barrel chest, flat stomach, and rough, rough skin, all so different from the tender muscularity of gym rats. Or maybe it's just the inward quality of his eyes, distracted by unknowable angers and affections, gnawing regrets and mysterious pleasures. Whatever it is, Jim Bridwell, the defining El Capitan climber of the 1970s, looks like he could kill you with his hands. There's an unnerving aura of physical power about the man, and weather, nicotine, and alcohol have worn his face into such a set mask of struggle, his straight white teeth clearly replacements, that if you met Bridwell in a bar and had the kind of active imagination I do, you'd guess he'd been a Green Beret in some Third World proxy war before settling into a civilian career of crimes high and low, multiple marriages, and lots of bar-fighting. In our age of climbers as airbrushed North Face athlete/models gleaming in the virtuous mountains, you wouldn't even consider that this man was the great American climber of his generation—perhaps the best in the world at his peak—and that he was absolutely still at it.

I met Bridwell at his home—one of the very few modest houses in all of Palm Springs. The thermometer had just hit a hundred and fifteen, with dry desert winds rattling hard over the dead brown Tehachapi Mountains, when I pulled off the highway and down the broad boulevards of grand resort hotels and retirement communities, the this-worldly afterlife of moneyed Southern California. Millions of gallons of High Sierra snowmelt sprayed

Jim Bridwell and friends.

into the furnace-like atmosphere, gushing over grand, pointless fountains, down fake, boulder-lined creekbeds, across square miles of immaculate Kentucky bluegrass lawn, and into the endless mist clouds of that city's restaurant and shopping mall humidifiers. Fifty-thousand-dollar automobiles were the norm, and the shopping district gleamed with gold-plated signage, at least until I turned onto Bridwell's circle-street in an older subdivision. Envy is a fault of mine—and I mean envy for just about everything that everybody else has—so I knew something about Bridwell before I even got out of the car. He doesn't have it, or at least not for money, because otherwise he'd go literally insane looking at the rewards of all that cash swirling around his simple home day after week after year. Outside, he had a beached trailer and a good old pickup, and inside, blankets covered all the windows (in the name of keeping cool) and several huge fans ran humming and loud, in lieu of air conditioning, keeping a constant hard breeze blowing around the shadows of the living room, not quite overwhelming the smell of cigarettes or the sound of a small, fiercely barking dog, or the cruel snorting of a big, mean, gray pig, a pet of his wife's that he confessed wanting to spit roast.

Bridwell wore his curly brown hair long in back, and faintly tinted eyeglasses in the style of an old hard-hat construction worker vacationing in the Bahamas. With a furtive, virile leer in his eyes, he lit a cigarette and started talking about how he'd spent the whole goddam day driving around trying to get someone to pay him for the use of some of his slides. He'd loaned them to a TV guy, and then the pictures just showed up on the tube, no payment forthcoming. Seemed Bridwell had tried to fight the thing out by representing himself in Small Claims Court, which meant trips all over the county, trying to make appearances and argue it out with some slick Los Angeles entertainment lawyer. ("I guess I'm not very good at being an asshole," Bridwell was saying, more or less to me. "Maybe if I was a better asshole.") Bridwell's conversation was peppered with stories like this, about the time he didn't get paid, or someone jilted him, or a French magazine lost his best slides. It seemed as though the passion of what he had done with his life had so consumed him as to remake him in its image—details had fallen by the wayside, bills, doubtless, had gone unpaid, calls unreturned.

Ten years younger than Robbins and twenty years younger than Harding, Bridwell was a military kid whose family moved around a lot. Spending much of his childhood in solitude, Bridwell found himself largely through sports—first as a baseball pitcher, and then with falconry when his family moved to California. At seventeen, Bridwell was looking through a guide to the national parks when he saw a two-page photograph of El Capitan and was "tantalized by its oceanic scale." He recalls deciding that he would one day climb it, and says that he saw a way up the thing even then, by way of the route that he would eventually follow on his first ascent of what he called Pacific Ocean Wall. It's awfully hard to imagine that a seventeen-year-old non-climber could pick out in a book photo the elusive sequence of ephemeral features that make up the adult master's Pacific Ocean Wall, but perhaps Bridwell just means he thought, "Wow, it would be awesome to climb that biggest, blankest part of El Cap, huh?" Either way, there's something compelling about this memory for Bridwell, suggesting an orderly destiny behind an otherwise perplexing life, proving the great signature route to be an inextricable function of who that climber is, a path he couldn't have not taken.

Soon after this revelation, Bridwell saw a photo of Layton Kor climbing Fisher Tower and was instantly sold on the sport; he went out rappelling the very next day on dirt mounds with a manila rope stolen from a transmission tower. Then he enrolled in a Sierra Club basic climbing course, and was immediately good at it, though he told Geoffrey Childs, in *Climbing* magazine, that "what I liked best about climbing was that I was accepted as myself." Upon his high school graduation, Bridwell was offered a track scholarship to Purdue, but turned it down to stay with his high school track coach at San Jose State. He went to Yosemite for the first time during the summer of his freshman year, and by the end of his sophomore year, in 1964, Bridwell had dropped out of school and headed to the valley for good. Soon, Bridwell had fought his way into the inner sanctum of Valley climbers, and in 1967, in anticipation of someday needing to rescue climbers off of El Capitan, the National Park Service commissioned Bridwell with creating and managing a high-angle rescue team in the Valley, to base itself in Camp 4, thus making him the original Duke of Yosemite climbing's only meaningful Dukedom. ("Not the wisest policy decision we ever made," a later park superintendent once said.)

Camp 4 had become, by then, an increasingly wild place. Kevin Worral recalls it as a kind of hobo heaven, "a community in every sense of the word," with "neighbors, love affairs, slums, parties, gymnasiums, loonies, territorial disputes, degeneration, and inspiration." Worral writes about climbers moving in for months at a time, thoroughly furnishing their campsites with carpets and kitchen cabinets, even running wires from the bathroom light fixtures for pirated electricity. The cultural revolution of the late 1960s was also having its effect on Camp 4 as, according to Childs, "the beat poetry, mountain chablis, and bongos of the 1950s had been replaced by Maharishi Yoga, blotter acid, and fuzzy riffs on cheap guitars." ("We were using hallucinogens," Bridwell

Sibylle Hechtel, first all-female ascent, the Nose.

told Childs, "to help us understand what we were experiencing from a point of view seldom visited by the western mind. We were trying to make sense of this new awareness. To unfold the mysteries. Drugs were equipment.")

Nobody was more emblematic of Camp 4's wildness than Bridwell himself. Childs recounts rumors of Bridwell's booting a tourist's barking poodle off Glacier Point, limping through a foot race with a sprained ankle and a Camel cigarette during the filming of "Battle of the Fittest" for television, and going one night with his friend Kim Schmitz to the home of a woman who had broken Schmitz's heart, spending a few hours shot-putting televisions, radios, and stereos and other household electronics through the window in a contest of strength, before "Schmitz concluded that they were in the wrong apartment." Another story has Bridwell finishing the first-ever coast-to-coast traverse of Borneo and coming down with something diagnosed as either liver flukes or stomach cancer; Bridwell apparently decided to burn the thing out of himself with alcohol, and eventually went to the toilet where "a ghastly worm the size and girth of a king snake slithered out of his anus." As Childs puts it, "Jim Bridwell may not have invented the low-ride, but anybody who has been in Yosemite and pushed their personal limits, stolen food off a tourist's tray, offended public decency, got drunk at their picnic table, played out their stay on crackers and relish, or slithered onto a half-driven RURP two thousand feet above the barbecued air of El Cap Meadow has stood along the banks of the river Bridwell and wondered at his beauty."

In the meantime, Bridwell was also dominating Yosemite climbing, handpicking the members of the gang that became the Search and Rescue team, setting a record for the highest number of Yosemite first ascents, and doing in a single two-week period in 1975 both the first one-day ascent of

El Capitan, with John Long and Billy Westbay, and the first ascent of Pacific Ocean Wall on the southeast face of El Capitan. Over the next decade, Bridwell not only set standards for free climbing in Yosemite, but put up one El Capitan route after another that redefined big wall climbing, including extreme outings like Sea of Dreams and Zenyatta Mondatta. The climbing on these routes was of a very peculiar kind—aid, to be sure, with forward progress made by standing in stirrups clipped to gear that has been driven into the rock, but with an increasingly desperate quality. The classic El Cap lines of the 1960s followed prominent crack systems, meaning that Robbins and Harding, when they weren't bolting, were usually driving pins. The incipient, elusive lines that were left to Bridwell's generation required more imaginative—and at times almost perverse—techniques. Committed to not placing bolts, and yet climbing smooth, steep terrain that still required use of a hammer, aid climbers of the seventies found themselves playing an increasingly strange game, like placing long strings of "bashies." Nothing more than lumps of copper or aluminum swaged onto a wire loop, bashies are placed against shallow little grooves— or even mere indentations—and then mashed into place with a hammer, their conformity to the rock providing their only holding power. On rock too sheer or blank for even bashies to hold, skyhooks came into wider use—curved bits of metal set delicately on minute edges, the leader easing his weight carefully, gently upwards, only to set another one. Where no edges would hold hooks, and earlier teams would have placed bolts, dowels came into vogue: little nubs of cylindrical aluminum stock driven as little as a quarter of an inch into shallowly drilled holes, and really a way of making even bolt placements tenuous.

Such equipment will not, by and large, hold more than the leader's bodyweight, and the aid rating system reflects this: A1 means that the gear is

easy to place and will hold a truck; A2 is harder to place and less secure; an A3 placement will hold only a short fall; A4 means that the gear is tricky to place and will not hold a fall at all; and A5, of which Sea of Dreams originally had twelve full pitches, involves such long strings of body-weight-only placements that pulling any single one will likely pull all of them, sending the leader on a fall of up to three hundred feet or more. This kind of climbing is also excruciatingly slow, a single hundred-and-fifty-foot pitch sometimes taking an entire day. Each placement requires ingenuity and an obsession with detail, and sudden movements can be fatal; Sea of Dreams has a notorious if-you-fall-you-die section, in which A5 climbing takes the leader high above a rock ledge. The experience has been likened to the meticulous defusing of a time bomb.

To hear Bridwell talk now about these climbs and those years is to hear the thoughts of a man inhabiting a parallel universe, one in which the kingdom hangs on whether Bridwell or someone else first thought of using bashies, and what exactly was their intended first use. He knows who first thought of hooks (himself, apparently) long before Chouinard began manufacturing them; who first thought of rivets and dowels and other devices, and exactly how they were used by whom and on what climb, as if this were the precise history of the early days of aviation. (Bridwell is still utterly obsessed with climbing hardware, in fact, still making much of it in his garage, picking up a cast-off bicycle inner tube in the street to show me how you can make quick-draw keepers by cutting it to pieces.) He knows the kinds of details about every one of his own El Cap routes—and every route he's ever done, for that matter—that only career fighter pilots know about planes, that only professional basketball players can tell you about a single pass made in a single game ten years before. He knows, for example, exactly who led which pitch,

Jim Bridwell, Pacific Ocean Wall.
following spread: Frank Sacherer, Camp 4.

whether that pitch was harder or easier than pitches Bridwell himself led; he knows who complained about what and exactly when, who did their share of the work; he knows the high points and climbing styles of every pre-Harding party on the Dawn Wall, including exactly which bolt on that overhanging face was placed by the hands of none other than John Harlin, a legendary American climber of an earlier era. For every one of his own climbs, Bridwell knows exactly how many holes he drilled on the first ascent and how many were for hooks, rivets, and bolts.

For the entire generation to follow Bridwell—a generation largely mentored and nurtured by him—Bridwell will even tell you exactly which route he first took them on, which moves they floundered on, and what tips he finally had to dole out. In a slide show he gives about Argentina's Cerro Torre, Bridwell recounts every attempt prior to his own, and meticulously compares weather patterns—the Americans, for example, who got an unprecedented fourteen days of good weather, and still couldn't do the climb. The heart of the slide show is given over to the Italian climber Antonio Maestri, who claimed to have made the first ascent of Cerro Torre. Bridwell demonstrates exactly where Maestri's bolt ladder stopped on the main headwall, eighty feet from the summit, surmises that Maestri couldn't possibly have finished by other means, and claims the mountain's first ascent for himself.

To a large degree, this is raw competitiveness. Climbing is, at its secret heart, a fiercely competitive sport. Most climbers do it privately without ever publicizing their exploits, but very few are those who won't eventually find a way to let you know what they've climbed, and fewer still are those who won't track the achievements of whichever climbers they consider their peers. In separate interviews with Bridwell, Mayfield, and Charlie Row, for example, the complete first ascent team for Zenyatta Mondatta, each climber told me with quiet pleasure that he personally had led the hardest pitches on the route. There should be no mystery about this: the pitches are very precisely rated for difficulty, and no mistake can be made about who led which. (Mayfield, I should note, immediately clarified by saying that while he personally led the greatest number of hard pitches, Bridwell had actually led the hardest single pitch.) This impulse towards self-assertion, it seems to me, is inescapable in a sport in which a person's greatest achievements go essentially unwitnessed, and unremembered unless he makes a personal point of turning them into history. Years later, nobody knows how good you were, and they'll never know unless you tell them or they repeat one of your routes.

This must have been especially galling in Bridwell's era, when El Capitan was simply no longer what it had been for Harding, Robbins, Chouinard, Frost, and the others. In a 1970 essay entitled "Coonyard Mouths Off," Chouinard wrote that El Capitan might have been "a spaced-out adventure once, when the odds were more stacked against you, but it's not such a big deal anymore." For the average, mortal climber, El Cap is still a plenty big deal, but for Chouinard's and Bridwell's peers, this was true: El Capitan had become terra cognita, and Chouinard was quite right that climbers of lesser ability were now regularly ascending the routes on which Chouinard's generation had once proven everything about themselves. This can't have felt good, diminishing as it did the achievements of an earlier time, and it also reflects what happens when something becomes known.

Take the example of Chuck Kroger and Scott Davis, two Stanford students who wanted to do the first ascent of the Dawn Wall in early 1970. Seeing Jim Bridwell's ropes on the climb (Harding hadn't come along yet),

following spread: Summit party.

they picked out the Heart Route instead, up overhung terrain to the right of the Salathé line. Because the earlier generation had already demonstrated that El Capitan could be climbed in good alpine style, Kroger has said, "with nothing to prove, we simply planned to have a good time." According to Steve Roper, over eight days of impeccable climbing, they named a white, towerlike formation "Tower to the People" in order to avoid the unsavory connotations of "White Tower," and they named one pitch "A5 traverse," even though it was much easier; they said they figured every El Cap route had to have an A5 traverse, so theirs would too—an El Capitan first ascent team is in dialogue, now, with those who have gone before. Far from the high seriousness of Robbins's accounts, Kroger described the experience as "like being dead for a week." Just below the summit, he apparently told Roper, Kroger carefully combed his hair before emerging onto the top, just so that "Royal and everyone else on the summit would like me. Then I stepped onto level ground. No one in sight . . . so we started running around looking behind trees and boulders, screaming, 'all right, you guys, we know you're up here somewhere.'" Nobody was waiting. The anecdote is meaningful for its awareness of climbing as authorship—not writing new meaning on a blank world, but rather participating in an ongoing conversation. It is an awareness, really, of being in the generation that came after.

Or, consider the example of Charlie Porter, who put up some of the greatest El Capitan routes of the post-Harding-Robbins era, including Mescalito and Tangerine Trip, the line Robbins had tried at the end of his career. Although Porter went on to staggering accomplishments in the far-off mountain ranges of the world, and once paddled a kayak around Cape Horn, the deed of a single day stands out in his Yosemite career. In 1972, on the Shield Route, Porter most amazed the Valley crowd not by the act of ascending a new swath of El Capitan, already a diminished grail, but by placing thirty-five RURPs in a single pitch while doing so. Realized Ultimate Reality Pitons are flat, postage-stamp-sized pieces of iron with wire loops swaged through a hole on one side; hammered into a hairline fracture or seam in the rock, they'll hold bodyweight but not, in all likelihood, a fall, meaning that if one comes out, they'll all come out. In other words, by the time Porter neared the end of that RURPing marathon, he faced the potential for a fall of somewhere around two hundred and forty feet, assuming his placements were four feet apart. To lead such a pitch can take as long as eight hours, an entire, exhausting day passed in a delicate play with gear over no more than a hundred and fifty feet of stone. The belayer waits patiently below, watching the shadows change, while the leader lives for hour after hour with the omnipresent possibility of an extremely long fall. A classic photo from perhaps the greatest climb of the era, published in George Meyers's *Yosemite Climber*, shows Dale Bard laughing in astonishment at one of the belay anchors during the first ascent of Sea of Dreams with Bridwell. Having just jumared a desperately hard pitch, taking out the marginal gear left by the leader, Bard has just discovered that he has been bouncing away in space on a rope secured to a string of RURPs tapped into a hairline seam. The look on his face? Pure, unalloyed joy.

● ● ●

There is, however, another way of viewing Bridwell's relentless assertion of the character of his climbs. Yvon Chouinard, long after his active years of Yosemite climbing, once likened the plotting of a big wall first ascent to an artist's plotting of a sculpture in a block of rock. Doug Robinson has likewise described a new route's execution to the actual creation of that sculpture, with the route's line and style constituting its aesthetic appeal. No climber has ever been lauded for establishing a route that wanders up and down various sides and buttresses of a mountain in order to express the chaos and point-lessness of late twentieth-century life, but climbs do have aesthetic meaning. The Salathé Wall, for example, meanders all over El Capitan's southwest face because Robbins, Pratt, and Frost were determined to reduce the use of bolts by linking naturally climbable features; their route, as a result, really does express a belief about an ideal way of being in the world, even a message about the sometimes hopeless path life seems to offer us, and the divine-seeming perfection of its resolution, at least for those with the faith to keep on seeking. Harding's Wall of the Early Morning Light and Nose, quite by contrast, derive their aesthetic appeal from precisely the opposite: the amount of time spent on each, the horrendous amount of drilling, and their diret-tìssimo quality—drawing straight lines up great swaths of rock.

The hard aid lines of the 1970s and early 1980s, however, are more difficult to appreciate—much the way twentieth-century abstract art will never speak to the masses like French Impressionism will. This is partly because of what they actually communicate—a nearly deranged lust for the edge—and partly because the appreciation of a Bridwell route can only be had in repeating it. And this is why, all these years later, when I sit in Jim Bridwell's living room and ask about the experience of those grand climbs, those great achievements of his glory days on El Capitan, Bridwell can barely bring himself to talk about them. Greg Child did Pacific Ocean Wall in the summer of 1977, and he describes it as a "sea of calms and swells along the

West Coast," and as "the epitome of the epitome" of El Capitan routes. "We were modern Michelangelos," Child writes, "and worked gently and carefully, regarding each placement like a crucial work of art, of copper and steel on granite." The comparison is apt, but incomplete. Imagine a sculpture that can only be known by hammering a chisel into its curves and lines, feeling what the creator must have felt—a sculpture, in other words, that can only properly be known by means that destroy it. Adding to the irony, the harder a climb is, the more true this becomes. Repeating one of Bridwell's routes, a climber might find himself at a place where the master—in his total commitment to craft—took chances this follower simply can't bring himself to do, placed yet another tentative hook while a fall to that ledge below becomes ever more certainly fatal. The sporting solution for the man who won't or can't do what his trailblazer has done is to retreat from the route and declare defeat. This requires a tremendous egolessness, however, and is far less likely than a furtive resort to the drill. The added hole, however, or even a simple enhancement to a hook placement in the middle of Bridwell's masterpiece, diminishes the difficulty of the climb and forever diminishes Bridwell's legacy. The artwork becomes, quite literally, defaced, impossible to see or know in its original form.

And so the only thing Bridwell can say now, and this with palpable bitterness, is that not a single climb of his has ever been repeated without additional hammering; not a single one, in other words, stood even a single new ascent without being degraded. Pacific Ocean Wall, he recalls, got *seventeen* new holes on its second ascent. He hissed the number like an outrage. Sea of Dreams, he says, only had thirty-nine holes originally. "We did a damn good job up there," he remembers angrily.

How many holes does it have now?

"Over two hundred."

Such a tremendous legacy, and all, in Bridwell's mind, at age fifty-four, "butchered," leaving a man with two options. Number one, let go, which Bridwell has tried to do by refusing to repeat any of his great routes, thus avoiding what could only be awful experiences; and number two, keep making a new legacy. Lurching up from the sofa, as if lurching away from the thought, Bridwell crossed the room and flipped through some books on a nearby table, produced a manila folder, and showed me what kept life feeling fresh: projects still harder, wilder, more dangerous than those he had done even in his twenties. And not just the Bear's Tooth in Alaska—a five-thousand-foot big wall route, with horrendous aid and mixed ice and snow climbing, which he'd just completed—but next year's project too. Earlier in the conversation, Bridwell had railed against the idea that a certain American climber was now considered the best in the world. "Because," Bridwell said, "sure, he's the best, except for maybe fifty German guys, about twenty Italians, maybe, I don't know, ten Spaniards . . . there's Russians who could climb circles around [the American in question]. This thing the Russians just did in the Himalayas? That's the cutting edge of world climbing." He paused then to show me a photograph of a massive unclimbed wall of snow and ice just to one side of Everest, a notoriously dangerous—even suicidal—labyrinth of rock chutes and avalanche gullies. "Course, we hope to change all that," he said, pointing out his proposed route, "when we get over there next year. After that, I'm going to retire."

following spread: Charlie Row, South Seas.

chapter

3

John Middendorf and Mike Corbett, two of the most
committed El Capitan climbers
of the post–Bridwell era, both arrived in Yosemite at the height of Bridwell's
reign. Like Bridwell, they were soldier's sons, though of very different back-
grounds. Where Corbett's father served two tours in Vietnam and came
home a disillusioned Democrat, Middendorf's father was Secretary of the
Navy. A gangly, long-limbed man of nearly forty, with an utterly disarming
face, Middendorf grew up in McLean, Virginia, started climbing while in
boarding school, and became the youngest guide at the Telluride Mountain
School before majoring in engineering at Dartmouth. Corbett, a short, stocky
man with a Yosemite Sam mustache and a gentle, self-effacing demeanor,
had been to nine different schools by the time he graduated from San
Francisco's George Washington High, and he never went to college at all—
just quit his first job after six months and moved right to the Valley. Corbett's
parents had split up long before, leaving his mother and sister well out of
touch back in Houston and his brother in the Eighty-Second Airborne out
of Fort Bragg, North Carolina. Soon after moving to Yosemite, Corbett lost
contact with his family altogether, so much so that they thought he was dead
for about the next twenty years. Letters they sent never reached Corbett, and
he didn't write or call.

By the late 1970s and early 1980s, the climbing world was primarily
focused on the more immediate pleasures of short free routes. But when
Middendorf took a summer off boarding school, borrowed his sister's car, and
drove it straight across country to Yosemite, entering the Valley on a moon-
lit night, he spent half an hour just staring up at El Cap, wondering if he'd
ever be good enough to climb the thing. In a two-week trip, Middendorf

Mike Corbett and Mark Wellman, the Shield.

crammed in a handful of big climbs, including Half Dome—waiting at the bottom of which he'd watched a bottle thrown off the summit explode a few feet away from him, then saw another climber fall eighty feet to the ground and break a leg. A few years later, he had transferred from Dartmouth to Stanford in order to be closer to Yosemite—only to find none of the valley locals interested in climbing big walls with him. So, he took up roped soloing, first on The Prow, in 1980, and then on Zodiac. Roped soloing is a system by which a lone climber belays himself, leading upwards while anchored below. At the end of a pitch, the climber builds a second anchor, rappels to the previous one, and then jumars back up, cleaning the pitch as he goes. He climbs the entire route, in effect, twice, and rappels the entire route once; he does absolutely all of the leading himself, and also all of the hauling, and performs a somewhat extreme exercise in self-reliance. Leading the second pitch of Zodiac, Middendorf was experimenting with a new self-belay system when he fell and had what he calls his first experience with time slowing down. Falling as fast as gravity would take him, he says he realized he was going to hit the ground, so he grabbed a loop of rope out of the air and wrapped it behind his back and got two huge grooves burned into his arm and body as he smacked into the wall, holding himself in a body belay. It's an astonishing claim, stretching the bounds of credibility, and yet clearly the story is not fiction. Realizing he was going to be in a lot of hurt in a big hurry, Middendorf says he rappelled to the ground, lay down in the sun, and couldn't move for two hours because he was in so much pain, crying and watching people bathe in the Merced. A few nights later, a pretty girl named Lydia crawled into Middendorf's hammock, changed his life forever, and earned a place at his side on his return to the Zodiac.

Pete Takeda, Sunkist.

Corbett, on the other hand, had been up El Capitan in the neighborhood of twenty-five times by 1984, with almost as many different partners. He told me there were about five years there when "people used to kid me that I should just get my mail up [on El Cap], 'cause I was up there all the time, and I don't know what that was all about except I just enjoyed it. It was real peaceful, it beat working, it was better than anything else I had going." And while Corbett was ratcheting up his El Cap climbing—by January of 1985 he would reach thirty—Middendorf, who had climbed the wall only half a dozen times, was ready to go cold turkey. One man was still burrowing into a world apart from his family; the other, feeling the tug of his family's expectations. Upon his graduation from Stanford, Middendorf sold all his climbing gear, sent out applications for mechanical engineering jobs, and was on his way to Montana when he made the mistake that probably redirected the rest of his life: stopping off in the Valley for one last look. Within a few days, Middendorf had landed a place with Corbett on Search and Rescue, by that time, the only way to camp in the valley for free, with no limit to your stay. While participating in technical high-angle rescues, team members made about $14 per hour, averaging around $2000 per year, and they saw ghastly, unforgettable things. Middendorf, for example, participated in the body-recovery operation of a woman who'd done over a thousand airplane jumps, but chose El Cap for her first parachute jump off fixed ground. Airplane jumping, Middendorf told me, is the easier sport, because you are already at high enough speed to control your movement, and there is also nothing to hit. Jumping off a fixed point like El Cap, he said, one can't steer for the first few seconds—until a certain speed is reached. According to Middendorf, this woman "back-slipped" towards El Cap without realizing it, and El Cap

Tower took off the top half of her head before she could pull the cord.

During those years, Middendorf froze in the winters in his lousy Jansport tent, put up six new big routes, and survived by rigging ropes for television ad-shoots and scrounging leftovers from cafeteria tables. When the tent got too cold, he bought a 1971 VW camper van with no engine and used it as a cottage in the parking lot. He describes those years as socially challenging, in the sense that it was pretty hard to meet girls. Most of his time was spent alone, on what Middendorf now sheepishly admits they called the Three Day Plan: one day to get ready, one day of free soloing on LSD, and one day to recuperate. Both Corbett and Middendorf put up new routes on El Capitan, some of them quite difficult—including Middendorf's A5 Atlantic Ocean Wall and Corbett's A5 On the Waterfront—but none that ascend new terrain from bottom to top. There simply weren't any top-to-bottom routes left, which is probably why a kind of malaise pervades the memories of wall climbers from this period. Dale Bard, the great El Capitan obsessive of the 1970s, and one of Bridwell's partners on Sea of Dreams, says he began putting up new routes simply for the pleasure of visiting certain places on the wall. Greg Child established two of the best routes of the 1980s—Aurora, which is a long variation on Charlie Porter's Tangerine Trip, and Lost in America, which joins Bridwell's Zenyatta Mondatta near the rim. Child describes the moment when he ran out of unclimbed terrain on Lost in America as like reaching "a place of dead roads." He also laments the democratic *festschrift* that had taken over the naming of El Capitan routes. In his book *Mixed Emotions*, Child recalls Robbins's outrage over the drug-tinged names of the 1970s, like Tangerine Trip and Magic Mushroom, names that so clearly signalled a generational shift away from the high-seriousness of Robbins's 1960s. Child decries the then-contemporary rise in names like Wyoming Sheep Ranch, which he sees as "a gauche slap-in-the-face nightmare of bestial images." Child is relieved only that the perpetrator, who has since left climbing for what Child calls a "Faustian pact with money" on Wall Street, failed to climb a line next to the Sheep Ranch and name it "Iowa Pig Farm," as he apparently intended.

The druggy 1970s, in other words, have given way to the money-crazed 1980s, and to their attendant post-modern failure of meaning, their inability to see any great endeavor as other than comic and pointless. Witness the names of Middendorf's and Corbett's own contributions to El Capitan: while in the tradition Child prefers, they clearly broadcast their late place in history. The Atlantic Ocean, after all, is measurably smaller than the Pacific Bridwell claimed (itself derivative of Robbins's North America), and Middendorf's route shares terrain with an older route that was itself already in an ironic dialogue with the foregoing route names: New Jersey Turnpike. Likewise Corbett's On the Waterfront—a variation both in name and terrain of the old Waterfall route.

Corbett's and Middendorf's big wall careers overlapped most closely in March of 1986, when they set out with Steve Bosque to repeat Warren Harding's route on the south face of Half Dome. In the early hours of their fourth day on the wall, while they slept in porta-ledges on the sheer face, a storm hit the team with high winds and rain, and Corbett's porta-ledge soon collapsed when moisture loosened its tensioning straps. According to Middendorf, Corbett got soaked to the skin while trying to rebuild his ledge, and then Middendorf's own ledge began to lose shape. Soon, he too—along with his sleeping bag—was as drenched as if he'd jumped into a lake. A foot-thick sheet of water was pouring down the face and rain was driving sideways in wind that, by dawn, had exceeded fifty miles per hour. Temperatures then dropped and their tangled ropes and other gear froze solid against the wall. Water-saturated piles of snow began to accumulate on the rain-flys of their tattered porta-ledges, such that Middendorf was nearly crushed by the weight. As the sun fell that day, with the storm still raging, Middendorf let himself fall asleep, and he recalls dreaming that he was in a boxing ring, being soundly thrashed by an array of opponents. He woke up to find Bosque standing on his head: seeing Middendorf's entire porta-ledge disappear under a pile of wet snow, Bosque and Corbett had climbed on top to dig him out. After that, in an effort to keep from falling asleep—which would surely have been fatal— Middendorf counted to 22,000 and made himself twitch with every number. By the next morning a rescue helicopter had found them.

In the aftermath, both Corbett and Middendorf redirected their lives. Middendorf, after moving to Arizona to get away from wall climbing, started the legendary A5 equipment company and reinvented porta-ledges in such a way that no future climber would ever suffer the way he and Corbett had. In 1989, Middendorf got back into wall climbing, and in 1992 he put his new porta-ledges to the test by heeding an old but famous call from Yvon Chouinard, who had declared that the real future of Yosemite climbing lay not in Yosemite but in applying Yosemite techniques to the "the great granite ranges of the world." Yosemite Valley, Chouinard once predicted, "will, in the near future, be the training ground for a new generation of super-alpinists who will venture forth to the high mountains of the world to do the most esthetic and difficult walls on the face of the earth." And so, the climb on which Middendorf now properly hangs his hat: not his El Capitan routes at all, but his Grand Voyage on Pakistan's Great Trango Tower.

With a three-thousand-foot snow and ice approach, and four thousand feet of hard aid and free climbing at high altitude, this climb is still considered one of the hardest big wall climbs ever done.

Corbett, for his part, got a janitorial job at the Yosemite medical clinic in order to pay off medicals bills incurred during his recovery from the Half Dome disaster. The job led to Corbett's first apartment, in the basement of the clinic, to a romance with a nurse, and to the drop in his annual El Cap rate to about twice a year (which brought him to forty-one ascents by 1987). It also led, in a roundabout way, to the opportunity that changed Corbett's life. In 1989, the very year in which Middendorf himself was getting back into wall climbing, Mark Wellman, a paraplegic Yosemite ranger, asked Corbett to take him up El Capitan. While planning the climb, building the customized gear, and developing the techniques for getting a paraplegic up the wall, Corbett also wrote a letter to Tom Brokaw at *NBC Nightly News*, a letter that was quickly answered with a request to film the whole climb. Corbett led the ascent, via Charlie Porter's Shield route, and Wellman, amazingly, pulled himself up ropes fixed by Corbett, doing the equivalent of seven thousand pull-ups. A little over half way, as a result of the television coverage, Corbett's girlfriend radioed up to say that his brother Tony had phoned. Corbett's mother, father, and sister, in their various cities, had all recognized Corbett on television, and nephews and nieces he'd never met were saying they would only eat cold bagels and cream cheese, because that's what they'd seen Uncle Mike eating. When they finally scrambled over the top, with Corbett actually carrying Wellman on his back, somewhere in the neighborhood of fifty reporters were waiting, including a helicopter television crew. Tom Brokaw actually interviewed them right at the edge of the cliff, for *NBC Nightly*

Sunkist bivouac.

News; in an exquisitely shameless twist, Brokaw had arranged for Corbett's sister and mother, whom he hadn't seen in twenty years, to participate in a three-way reunion interview.

From there, Corbett's story is one of escalating meaning. According to Wellman's memoir, *Climbing Back*, an unfamiliar woman approached Corbett on the trail that very afternoon. "Six years ago today," she told Corbett quietly, "on July 26, 1983, my son committed suicide in Yosemite. Every year on this date, I come back to Yosemite to think about my son. And every year I cry. But this year, because of what you two have done, I didn't cry. From now on, when I come back each year, I am going to celebrate the life of my son, instead of his death. You two inspired me to do that, and I just wanted you to know." During the climb, Corbett got a sliver of metal stuck in his cornea, and the doctor who removed it afterwards waived the fee—which would have bankrupted the still poor Corbett—in exchange for an autograph for his son. An audience with President Bush followed, en route to which a flight attendant announced the presence of Corbett and Wellman on the plane. A round of applause erupted from the passengers, and a steward brought a free bottle of champagne. In Washington, they were put up in the presidential suite at the Washington Hilton, and even Warren Harding called, asking to be taken up the Nose for the thirty-first anniversary of his first ascent, an experience Corbett puts ahead of meeting the president.

Still more good things followed, as Wellman threw out the first ball of an Oakland A's game, with Corbett at his side, and in April 1991, Corbett married a ranger he'd met through Wellman, with Wellman as his best man. "Looming directly above us," Corbett wrote of the ceremony, "as if it were the guest of honor, was my old friend, El Capitan." In a foreword to Wellman's book, then-Senate Republican Leader Robert Dole claimed an affinity to Wellman as a disabled American and compared Wellman's ordeal to his own ordeal of being wounded by German machine-gun fire in the mountains of northern Italy. Shortly after Wellman and Corbett finished their climb, Dole reported proudly, "the full U.S. Senate was voting on my resolution to commend them for 'their extraordinary feat of bravery . . . setting an outstanding example for all Americans and persons with disabilities.' The Senate isn't known for agreeing on much, but on this issue, it was unanimous." The nation, in other words, was united in its belief in the value of what Corbett and Wellman had done.

But greater than all those kudos was the final twist with Corbett's family: someone at Continental Airlines saw Brokaw's interview and arranged to fly the entire Corbett clan to Yosemite for free. Corbett recalls much change: everyone looked older, for one thing, and he had five nieces and nephews; perhaps most significant, his once overpowering father had had six strokes and was clearly quite disabled. In Wellman's book, Corbett describes the pleasure he felt upon discovering that both of his siblings had named their firstborns after him, and that while his father said little that day, he followed every-where, staying close to Corbett's side and listening carefully. "At lunch," Corbett remembers, "he took the seat right next to mine, and he leaned close to hear every word I said." At one point, Corbett writes, "I compli-mented my dad on his watch, and he slid it off his wrist and gave it to me."

• • •

And now? Well, Middendorf did about ten more walls in the years after Grand Voyage, but his interest cooled after the loss of a few friends and the realization that, as he put it, "I was up to a level of wanting to put my life on a fifty-fifty kind of line." Then there'd been a period of cliff and bridge jumping, with standard climbing ropes. Driving me up to Yosemite one evening, Middendorf talked about a bridge jump he'd done nearby, how he didn't land right—this was back in the eighties, before they'd even thought of using chest harnesses, and his back bowed and popped a few times. He was dangling on the bottom for a long time, thinking he'd broken his back, and by the time he'd jumared to the top again he could barely move. Then a friend jumped, but caught a piece of gear on a bridge bolt and hung there screaming, "Help! Help! I'm going to suffocate! My ribs are breaking! I'm going to die! Oh God, help me, Deucey, help!" Limping over in pain of his own, Middendorf pulled the guy up enough to free him from the bolt.

A passing motorist heard the screaming and stopped his car, ran to the bridge edge, and looked off just in time to see Middendorf let his friend plummet. The poor motorist turned to Middendorf and said, "He's dead, isn't he?"

"No," Middendorf replied, "we're actually just goofing off."

"That's a helluva way to have fun," the man retorted, enraged. "I'm going to go call the cops right now."

Well, that meant Middendorf's friend had to do a lickety-split jumaring job—and they slipped out just as those whirling colored lights came around the bend.

And just that May, Middendorf and the late Dan Osman had jumped off a bridge in Glen Canyon, with a 467-foot drop in a canyon only 200 feet wide. Because rope jumps require you to jump off to the side of your anchor—so as not to squarely impact the rope—Middendorf had to jump quite close to the cliff face. Over the five seconds of freefall, the wind blew him closer and closer to the canyon wall, until he was no more than twenty feet from it. Just before he would have been torn apart, the wind shifted again, and drew him back to safety. When he came to rest, he hung fifteen feet from the canyon floor.

"That sounds intense," I said, a little unnerved.

"Yeah," Middendorf admitted, "it was actually a little too intense."

In fact, in the time since, Middendorf has gotten to work at reinventing himself yet again. He has sold his A5 Outfitters to The North Face, taken courses at Harvard in the architecture of tension fabric structures, and hurled himself into an environmental legal battle over the future of the Yosemite climbers' campground. He's become active in the American Alpine Club—giving back to the sport that has given him so much—and has moved once again to Arizona, where this world-class climber has somehow landed work as a Colorado River rafting guide in the Grand Canyon.

• • •

And Corbett? The only man since Warren Harding to have become nationally famous for climbing El Capitan, Corbett has now lived in Yosemite Valley continuously for twenty-four years, and he has business cards that say "Mr. El Cap," as well as a large home collection of historical, El Capitan–related equipment, ephemera, letters, newspaper clippings, and magazine articles. He has climbed El Capitan nearly sixty times over thirty years, with forty-six different partners via twenty-five different routes, for an average rate of once every four months. He has, in fact, climbed the wall twice in every month of the year except for March, in which he has only climbed it once. Corbett is so utterly immersed in the world of El Capitan that he could tell me over lunch that he really isn't obsessed with El Capitan, and never has been. ("I guess you can call it an obsession," he allowed a few minutes later, "I don't have any better word for it. There's nothing wrong with being obsessed, and to be obsessed is not really negative. People think of it as negative, but it's not, really. It's whatever floats your boat, I guess.") Corbett's family, as it turned out, only stayed in Yosemite for a couple of days after the Wellman climb, "but now we all write each other," Corbett said, "and drop by for visits when we can, just like a real family." Corbett has since guided Wellman up Half Dome, a much more arduous experience than their El Cap ascent, and in 1999 he took an eighty-one-year-old man up El Capitan. Taken together, these experiences have completely changed his relationship to climbing. "I don't like to strong-arm El Cap now," he told me. "Like, I would never even think about going up there in a strong team, get two other guys that have done it like thirty, forty times. What's the challenge? It's like getting El Cap in a headlock." He says he has more fun when his back's against the wall. "I would have made a good soldier," he told me, working on a cheeseburger and a Coke outside the Yosemite Mountaineering Store, at which he's a cashier. He said he just likes the way El Capitan focuses him, because, by his own admission, "I don't really pay much attention in life. I really only pay attention at the cash register and on the rock, because if you make mistakes at the register, you get fired, and if you make mistakes on the rock, you die."

"You know how I think about El Capitan?" Corbett asked me, a smile broadening on his face. "Kind of like . . . you know Linus and his blanket? You know, you're carrying around a little blanket, and he's always sucking his thumb and holding his blanket, and El Cap's kind of that way for me. Visitors will ask me how I sleep up there and I say, 'Like a baby! It's where I want to sleep.'"

following spread: Jeff Paria, eleventh pitch, Aurora.

chapter

4

One day in the summer of 1998, I drove up to Yosemite with John Middendorf.

We got to the Valley at dusk and pulled over for an obligatory hello to the Big Stone, then drove on to Camp 4, where crowds huddled around picnic tables, with lantern light on their faces and the sound of crickets clattering in the hot night, moonlight gleaming on the high white walls all around. We picked our way through the campground towards Bridwell's creation and Middendorf's former home, the Search and Rescue site, a collection of wood-framed canvas cabins at the back. As we approached, a banging din arose from two men beating pots together, shouting. A huge, dark animal appeared in my headlamp's beam, and then I realized a bear was scurrying back into the forest. At the home of Werner Braun, Search and Rescue member for over twenty years, we lay down our bags on the pine needles and prepared to sleep. As I drifted off, a wild crashing sound started, and then a man shouted in Spanish—the bear, again.

We woke up at dawn and walked through the campground, among sleeping bags and tents crowded everywhere, an open dormitory of the young, filthy, and driven. A few guys stood drinking coffee, their knees and hands horribly scabbed, their iron gear clanking in their fingers. A long line had already formed at the ranger's kiosk, among climbers trying to find a site. Soft grey light came down on the walls as we returned to the parking lot, where we found the back window of John's pickup camper shell absolutely shattered. More ursine mischief. A nearby Honda, one of several cars bearing A5 stickers, had suffered even worse: not only had the rear passenger window been shattered, but the frame of the door had been bent well away from the car. Middendorf's socks were scattered around the lot. A climber

Scott Burk, freeing the Nose.

Middendorf referred to as "e coli" walked up and called out to "Deucey" (dorf—Dusseldorf—Deucey), and said, "Yeah, dude, they really go for red Nissans. Sometimes even if you don't have food they'll just break in for good measure and leave a note saying Next time, Get some food." He recommended spreading dirty clothes all over the inside of the car, as a deterrent, said it really worked for him, at least.

We had breakfast with several men involved in a lawsuit to stop the National Park Service from building employee dormitories on Camp 4, including Tom Frost. Now sixty-one years old, Frost was slight of build, with snow white hair and an electric aliveness. He somehow combined a ferocious sense of purpose with a truly lighthearted manner.

I asked Frost if Camp 4 had changed much since the old days, and he said, "Sure! You can't hear any English spoken around here anymore." He clearly saw this as a marvelous development. "And all the Europeans are coming here still, because they have to do the classic routes. Chouinard once predicted that the great alpinists of the world would eventually come out of Yosemite, and it was true, but now it's also true that the great alpinists of the world have to *come* to Yosemite, from all over! It used to be just a half dozen Americans here—maybe a dozen—camping back up there in the trees. A few of us, and then some guys from Southern California, and Camp 4 was for people with pets back then, so we had to have the indignity of sharing the place with dogs. And we had a good rapport with the rangers, too—they liked what we were up to. And you know, I remember when we were up on the Salathé, there were no other climbers in the Valley, much less on El Cap, and we were talking about how, except for our families, nobody even knew we were there, and *nobody* had any clue what we were actually up to. And then last summer, when he went to do the Nose, there were six parties in queue! And then, of course, there was Spartacus."

"Spartacus?"

"The biggest bear in Yosemite. Chuck Pratt had an ongoing thing with Spartacus, where he finally stood on a boulder back there with a huge rock, waiting. Dropped it right on Spartacus's head as the bear passed by. The bear just kind of shrugged, looked around in confusion, and kept going."

"Because they were stealing food all the time?"

"Oh, we didn't mind sharing food with the bears. We understood the bears back then, and they understood us, and it was mostly just a battle of wits between us. But that thing Pratt had with Spartacus, that was different. That was personal."

After breakfast, we walked back to the campground and bumped into a big crowd of guys, including Conrad Anker, one of the great big wall climbers of the decade (who once blew past me on Half Dome—after three days of climbing, I was hunkered down at a bivouac called Big Sandy Ledge, when Anker and three other guys, having left the cafeteria that very morning at nine-thirty, romped past laughing and having a ball). Dan Osman was there, only several months before he died while jumping recreationally off the Leaning Tower, and so was an Englishman named Kevin Thaw, and a younger man named Miles Smart. They'd been up on North America Wall for three days, trying to free climb certain sections. Standing before Frost, one of the route's original authors, they were eager to pay their respects. Anker was telling Frost that the whole thing will "go free"—meaning yield to ascent by hands and feet only, with equipment used strictly as a safety net —except the "second pendulum," where they'd have to use a long diorite traverse that would probably just come off in the next freeze. "But man," Anker said, "that rock is *so* featured. Just square cuts." One member of the group, a man named Wally, had silver hair and silver eyes, a square-cut jaw, and massive hands. An accountant who spent all of his downtime on El Capitan, usually soloing desperate aid routes, he had just come off Steve Gerberding's A5 Reticent Wall after twelve days completely alone.

A young woman appeared nearby and asked about crapping on El Capitan, how exactly it was done. Middendorf reported that you were now supposed to bring a long PVC pipe with unscrewable end-pieces, crap in there and haul it along with you. Some guy apparently left his by some cars in El Cap meadow last year, however, and the bomb squad actually came out and blew the thing up, making a hell of a mess.

A young man aptly nicknamed "Linus" appeared then, with an equally scruffy and spaced-out partner who introduced himself as "Captain Kirk." In any other setting, they would have been taken for indigent and homeless, but they'd actually just been on an El Capitan route called South Seas for the last eight days. They'd run out of water with a day and a half to go, in hundred-degree heat, so they were pretty parched even now, a few days later, sucking Olde English Malt Liquor in the parking lot.

"Hey Deucey," Linus said to Middendorf, "you need to make your haul bags about two inches bigger."

"Deeper?"

"No wider, for a keg."

They'd hauled a full keg clear to Heart Ledges, it turned out, where they'd had a party with eighteen people on two different ledge terraces.

"That sounds kind of crowded."

"Yeah, it was tight. But anyone who seemed too buzzed, we took a Leatherman and ratcheted down his locker (carabiner) so he'd never get it undone alone."

"What was the party for?"

"Just had to be done."

• • •

A world, in other words, still thrives around El Capitan. New routes still go up—albeit all variations on older routes—and the culture still celebrates "firsts" of various kinds, like first solo ascents of existing routes, first one-day ascents, and first solo one-day ascents. "Big Wall Amy" Aucoin, a good-natured, attractive young woman, has been quietly doing first "all-female" ascents of some of the harder aid lines—she got sick of people approaching whatever guy she'd just guided up El Capitan, asking *him* what route they'd done, so she started a "women-only" rule for herself. Peter Croft and Hans Florine led separate partners in a series of speed duels on the Nose in the early 1990s, then teamed up and did the climb in well under five hours. "Link-ups" are likewise considered valid statements—Croft and John Bachar, for example, doing the Nose and the northwest face of Half Dome in a day, Florine and another partner doing three El Capitan routes in a day, and Florine and Dean Potter each soloing both the Nose and Half Dome in under twenty-four hours. By the time I caught up with Steve Gerberding, he had climbed El Capitan eighty-seven times. And yet, when I first approached him in the light-dappled shade of the Yosemite Lodge courtyard, saying I wanted to talk to people who'd spent a lot of time on El Cap, Gerberding's response was, "Oh, you've got to talk to Chris MacNamara. Mac's your guy." (I did eventually talk to MacNamara, and found a polite, intelligent young man who had somehow climbed El Capitan more than fifty times by the age of twenty, and all during breaks from his classes at UC Berkeley.)

To a Chouinard or a Robbins, I suppose, this might all diminish the wall, as the game takes on the internecine quality of a competition among ancient monks over who can copy out the most scripture. En route to his El Cap–Half Dome solo link-up, for example, Florine devoted much of a decade to climbing the Nose as fast as possible—which was awfully fast, given that for a few years Florine was the world speed climbing champion. First with Andres Puhvel, and eventually with Peter Croft, Florine whittled the time on the Nose down to four hours, twenty-two minutes. (On one of the pushes with Puhvel, Florine started climbing at about 5:00 A.M., while I was beginning to jumar lines I'd fixed to Sickle Ledge. An hour later, we all stood on Sickle Ledge together. Half the day later, I was in the middle of the Stoveleg cracks, freaking out and deciding to retreat. That night, I saw Puhvel in the Ahwahnee Hotel, mooching a free cup of tea. "Hey," Andy said, recognizing me, "you bailed! But you were doing so well! We saw you guys cruise the pendulum to the Stovelegs." Exactly where, I wanted to know, had they seen this from—the Great Roof? The Glowering Spot? "Actually," Puhvel said, "the meadow. We were back having lunch.")

As a result, Florine knows every single piece of gear, move of a hand, and rope trick he can pull on every single foot of Warren Harding's three-thousand-foot-long creation—a creation that Florine knows, in short, better than most people ever know anything in their lives. (Florine speaks of all this, incidentally, with a kind of goofy reverence—a breathless exuberance that conveys both delight and mystification with the direction his life has gone.) This also, however, demonstrates the depth of the great wall's allure—El Capitan simply does not get climbed out. Witness the push to free climb existing El Capitan routes—despite the hard work of the greatest climbers of the 1960s and 1970s, it wasn't until 1988 that Todd Skinner and Paul Pianna fought their way up the Salathé for the first completely free ascent of El Cap, and not until 1992 that Lynn Hill freed the Nose. Suddenly, El Capitan seems not exhausted but brand new.

Certainly it seems that way to Scott Burk, a tightly wound man in his late thirties, of medium height, with coarse muscles, heavily chiseled features, ferociously close-set eyes, and a rock-and-roller's bushy hair. Burk got climbing early, doing the northwest face of Half Dome when he was only fourteen, and he has been a fixture in the Valley ever since; more than twenty years later, he lives in a Search and Rescue tent cabin in Camp 4. "What's always bothered me about climbing, though," he told me, as we walked towards the Yosemite Lodge Cafeteria, "is that you can do something hard, and then right away you're like, 'Oh, I can't *imagine* what it would feel like to do *this*,' and then you do that too and the feeling's really not that huge." Passing the temporary employee housing, he bounced forward with each step—his walk saying, I'm going somewhere great, right now. "The feeling's big for a little bit," he said in a positive tone, "but then I started realizing, I realized years ago that I got to start doing stuff so sick that the feeling lasts longer, or otherwise I'm going to kill myself, as a manic depressive. I'll end up going out. And I did that in various ways over the years, through the use of drugs. I don't do that shit anymore, but ah . . ." His attention drifted for a moment, as if caught by a startling thought, and then he returned: "I realized that I was actually trying to kill myself, but a part of me wouldn't let me do it. Self-preservation kicked in." There's a chilling self-knowledge at the center of this, and one that casts an uncomfortable light on the lives of many climbers: the struggle is what feels good, not the achievement. "Once I realized what was happening," Burk said, "I'd been up in Tahoe for five straight winters, working as a ski tech. It was in '95, and I moved down here to stay every winter until I free El Cap— I gave myself something that was impossible. I've always done that."

In other words, Burk's idea of self-preservation in the face of a downward-spiralling life was a commitment to repeating Lynn Hill's achievement on the Nose. Burk was a very, very good free climber at the time, with impeccable Yosemite credentials and a lifetime's experience on Yosemite granite, but he wasn't a young man, and even when he was, he'd never been a climber of Lynn Hill's calibre. He had climbed the Nose in a day six times in six years, but he was still not the obvious candidate for second ascensionist of the hardest big wall free climb in the world. Much in the manner of Bridwell's claim to a boyhood vision of Pacific Ocean Wall, Burk gives meaning to this somewhat peculiar quest by placing its motivations outside the realm of competition. He'd been looking at freeing the Nose, he told me, since 1990, well before Lynn Hill even thought of it; by this, he meant not to take away from Hill's achievement so much as to give his own effort wholly to himself. To make the point even further, Burk then reconsidered: "Well, actually," he added, now leading the way into the cafeteria for breakfast, "the whole thing started even earlier. I started wanting to free the Nose before I even knew what climbing was. Yeah, I came as a little kid with my dad and I looked up at El Cap and I wanted to spiderman up it, and I knew even then that it could be done." He shook his head in disbelief, amazed at the prescience of his toddling self. "And the funny thing is," Burk added, "in some of my pictures from the latest free push I'm wearing red and blue, and it looks just like Spidey."

Scott Burk is wonderful company—warm-hearted, vulnerable, side-splittingly funny, and unfailingly polite. He is also a tremendous story teller, and his tale of his struggle to free the Nose is as much an achievement as his success. The way he tells it, the effort got off to a somewhat dilatory start. The Nose has three crux sections: the Great Roof, the short Changing Corners, which is the hardest of all, and the Summit Overhangs. In 1996, Burk says that he decided to start by tackling some of the lesser—but still quite difficult—sections below the Great Roof. With a partner named "Spaz," Burk says that he started at 9:00 P.M. one evening, freeing the first four pitches by 4:00 A.M. Back on the climb at 11:00 A.M. the next day, Burk was almost a third of the way up when he remembered he was supposed to start a new job cleaning floors at the Village Store that night, so he went down. His focus waned for a few months due to "girl problems," and by the time he returned in the late autumn, jumaring up lines left on his first attempt, intervening storms had littered the base of the wall with dead branches, rocks, dirt, and dead animals—Burk told *Rock and Ice* magazine that he even found half a peregrine falcon, chopped by falling ice.

The next summer, Burk decided to establish a camp on the top of El Capitan, from which to access the wall by rappelling down from above. First, he and a young climber named Chris set out hiking with several hundred pounds of supplies, but an unexpected snowstorm turned them back (as did Chris's confession that he was on Ritalin at the time—"Make sure I don't lose this shit," he apparently told Burk, "pot helps too"). While hauling gear up the more direct East Ledges route, they dropped a hundred-pound bag the full length of a static rope; Burk feels sure that it would have ripped the anchor out and taken them all to their deaths if the rope hadn't wrapped around Chris's foot and stopped dead—without, miraculously, tearing off Chris's foot. Then, while Burk worked out the moves of the route's over-hanging last pitch, Chris snapped. He had, apparently, set his heart on working the Great Roof pitch first, and as the hours passed his frustration boiled over. "Fuck you, Scotty," Burk recalls his screaming, "I'm quitting! I quit! I'm cutting these fucking ropes! I'm cutting everything!" Burk swung out from the wall and saw Chris approaching their third partner, who was holding the rope on which Burk's life depended. By the time he'd scrambled to the top, however, everything was peaceful again. "Bro," Chris said, his mood past, "it's cool, I'm back on the team." Two weeks later, Burk had climbed the final pitch on top rope ten times and downclimbed it once.

The next and greatest obstacle was Changing Corners, the twenty feet of climbing that Lynn Hill had described as "you climb up a crack, throw your hand out to an arete, then throw your foot onto the face and hope that it stays! Then match hands on the arete and get over into the corner. From there it's all strange climbing and weird stemming." Burk spent several weeks trying to find a variation, a way around the traverse Hill made, and in the process ripped open his fingers while trying to go from crack to crack, broke a key hold while trying to step across with his feet, and broke still more holds while trying to come in from a route next to the Nose. By this time, Burk was washing windows on weekends and spending up to six days a week living on top of El Cap in what had become a substantial encampment, with dinners of stir-fried vegetables or even steak, French-press coffee in the morning, and a five-gallon bucket of candy bars to keep his partners happy. He generally woke up at 4:30 A.M., made a fire, brewed coffee, and then went down the ropes to get started, making as many as four trips in a single day, for a total of twenty-four hundred feet of jumaring over the course of a sixteen-hour work day. "I'd push it until I was seeing colors," he told me. "There were times down there I didn't know where I was. Where I felt completely in jail. I felt like I was in a little corner in a cave and I couldn't get out. When you're actually at your limits on El Cap, it's crazy how you work. Harder than anyone could ever pay you to. For any amount of money. I would work until I'd be down there hanging and all of a sudden I would realize I was facing straight out, and looking at Middle Cathedral, and that I was afraid because I didn't think I could even get up the rope, and I couldn't get down. Totally dangling, and my partner would be just holding me."

The hardest part of the pitch involved moving out of one steep, smooth corner to another. The problem was that Burk couldn't even make the reach between the two. So, for weeks at a time, he worked simply at stretching his wingspan. "It took me three full weeks," Burk said, "before I could notice a difference. I noticed that I could get my second knuckle on one side and just barely on the other side." Eventually, he worked at hanging in the right position for minutes at a time, then at doing pull-ups where he once couldn't hang at all. Next came a series of interlocking, step-through knee-bars, a kind contortionist escape-artist act. The exhaustion of this sent Burk on a regime of upside down sit-ups done from within the knee-bar positions. After he could top-rope the pitch repeatedly, Burk got to work at leading it, but on his seventeenth try, he popped a tendon in his middle finger and took three weeks off, after which he did the pitch without falling.

Now four and a half months into the project, Burk decided to try a ground-to-summit attempt. With six hundred pounds of supplies preplaced on the route, he took off in late November. It snowed two feet in six hours on their first night on the wall, he told *Rock and Ice*, with "snow sloughs the size of buses sweeping the face, coming down over the porta-ledges," and continued the next day, too. On the following day, the snow on the summit had begun to melt, percolating down through El Cap until it was pouring out of the Great Roof, but Burk says he still managed to work on the Great Roof pitch for seven days, sopping wet and freezing cold in the shade, having his partner lower him into the sun to warm him up when he couldn't take it anymore. Burk had almost mastered the moves—the only moves standing between him and a run up through sections he had already worked out—when another storm dumped six feet of snow with 120 mph winds. Burk sat out the three-day blizzard in his porta-ledge, and when it stopped, and "we stuck our heads out, we were greeted by the most beautiful and terrifying landscape I'd ever seen. The whole upper face of El Cap," Burk recalls, "was encased in like a foot of solid water ice. There were twenty-five-foot-long icicles hanging off the Great Roof and dozens more off the top of El Cap, a thousand feet above us. Ice chunks the size of my Volkswagen bus were breaking off and hitting the wall above, below, and on both sides of us. The whole wall was shaking on impact. It felt like war. Loud, deadly war." The rappel lines were completely iced over, making retreat impossible, so Burk got on his cell phone and said good-bye to everyone he knew. "They were crying," Burk said, "and I was crying, and I was trying to hold it together." Then, on the fifteenth day on the wall, while Burk was boiling water inside his porta-ledge, the flame exhausted the little space's oxygen. He soon passed out, breathing butane until his partner heard him screaming and came over to see what was wrong, found Burk purple in the face and cold to the touch, with a chunk of ice lodged in his throat. Burk came to in a puddle of water (the spilled pot), and accepted defeat. By midafternoon, his rappel lines had unfrozen, so he tied inflated river bags all over himself for protection against falling ice and started for the ground. "By the time I reached bottom," Burk recalls, "I was bruised all over from ice shrapnel. Once I was on flat ground, I couldn't walk. Every time I tried to stand up, I fell over. I just lay at the bottom of El Cap and wept, staring at the death icicles overhead." Two friends, he says, came looking for him and it took them two and a half hours to get him back to the road.

Undeterred, Burk returned the following summer only to find that he could no longer climb Changing Corners. After another two months of total commitment, he was once again where he had left off the prior year, and then a crucial hold broke off. "I was so pissed," Burk told me with evident pleasure, "but in some ways I thought, 'All right, now it's even harder.'" Eleven days later, he found a way around the missing hold, got himself to the kneebar section, and climbed the whole pitch twice without falling. In October of 1998, almost three months into his third season of trying to free the Nose, Burk readied his summit camp for a victory celebration, preplaced three hundred pounds of bivouac gear, water, and food at Camp 4, and started from the ground. The Great Roof was so wet from a prior storm, with water still streaming down it, that Burk accepted the partial victory of climbing it on top rope. A storm was setting just as he reached what by now he was calling the Houdini Pitch—Changing Corners. High winds and cold air tore about him while he made the additional small compromise of clipping into preplaced gear, and that night the storm hit with hard rain and hundred-mile-per-hour winds. On the final mantel moves of the final pitch of his final effort to free the Nose from ground to top in a single push, water was running across the holds he had to use, so Burk dumped out two entire chalk bags on a single hold, soaking up enough water for just long enough to allow him to pull on through to the top.

"Anything this big," he said by way of explanation, "anything that takes this much time and effort, it has to have immense underlying value. I know that as long as I stay with it, I will find that value."

following spreads: Chris McNamara and Miles Smart, speed climb of Zodiac.

I climbed the wall one more time

in the summer of 1992

—via the Nose, with a New Zealander named Peter Woolford whom I'd met in Berkeley's Marmot Mountain Works, where I was then a climbing shoe repairman. We did the route in standard time, and it was an enormous help to know from firsthand experience that El Capitan actually had a top. In fact, I felt so at peace over those four days that I decided that climbing El Cap would become a regular pastime for me, too, as it clearly was for Steve Gerberding. I imagined myself taking long weekends at age fifty just to go knock off yet another El Cap route—that I would spend as much time as I could toiling pointlessly in the sky. I actually called up Middendorf and ordered a full complement of the specialized gear he made for "nail-up" routes like Mescalito and Pacific Ocean Wall, and I began to find exquisitely roundabout ways of letting even nonclimbers know that I had climbed El Capitan, somehow bringing it into virtually every conversation I had. ("You surf here often?" a guy might ask. "Oh, yeah, I guess I do these days. Now that I'm on the coast so much more." "Were you living somewhere else?" "No, I just used to spend most of my time up in the mountains." "Really? Doing what?" Or, a real favorite: "Well, I was rock-climbing a lot for the last few years, but I recently did this one, big climb I'd been working towards for a long time." "Oh, really, which one was that?")

My Louisiana-born-and-bred girlfriend didn't quite get how impressed she was supposed to be, so I actually drove her up to Yosemite to show her the thing—her first ever visit to proper mountains. Stopping at El Cap

The Nose.

meadow, after the long drive from the coast, I pulled her out of the car, pointed, and waited—waited for her jaw to fall, gob-struck, and for me to loom suddenly larger in her eyes. I bounded around in my excitement, thrilled as ever to be below the thing myself, right up until I noticed that it was having absolutely no effect on this girl at all. In retrospect, I'm sure I had simply oversold the thing, ruining any possibility of a genuine response on her part. At the time, I figured she just needed some help. We happened to be standing in the tall grass near a German man who had a pair of binoculars, so I asked if I could borrow them. I hoped to pick out a climber somewhere on the wall, show the climber to my girl, and thus make a last-ditch effort to impress upon her the wall's magnificent scale (and thus my own magnificence, by association).

"People climb this thing?" the man asked, when he divined my intentions.

"They sure do."

"I can't believe that," he said, quite firmly.

"It's true," I insisted. "I'll find someone here in a minute."

"No, that can't be," the man declared with great finality.

"I've actually climbed it myself," I said, lowering the binoculars from my eyes.

"You've got to be joking," he replied, breaking into a broad grin. "No, no, I don't believe that for one moment."

"Really," I insisted, now getting a little irritated. "I've climbed it twice."

"That's preposterous," the man told me, right to my face. "You've done no such thing. Now give me back my glasses and I'll be on my way." With that, he took his binoculars and stormed off.

When I turned to my girl, she could scarcely suppress a giggle.

That very afternoon, however, we bumped into Steve Gerberding by the side of the road—a coyote, he seemed to me, so self-confident and so inalienably cool. He asked generously if I'd been "up on the Big Stone" lately, and I was thrilled to answer in the affirmative, feeling that I had taken yet another small step down what I saw as a whole new, vastly longer and more serious path. I even asked the same of Gerberding: "How about you? Been back up there?"

"Bunch of times," he said. "Yeah."

Then I asked a question I immediately regretted: "You never get tired of it, huh?"

I'm still not sure what I was asking. Will *I* ever tire of it? Maybe. Or, perhaps I already sensed the passion slipping away from me, and knew that I would never become half the climber that Gerberding was, or even a climber he might consider a peer. Perhaps I was uncomfortable with this, caught in a wavering moment between one code of self-evaluation and the next, arguing it out in my head. Whatever I meant, I hinted, albeit vaguely and unintentionally, that Gerberding had done something questionable with his time in this world.

Gerberding, of course, just shook his head and said, "Nope, I never do get tired of it. It's too big."

Photography Credits

Chris McNamara, Tangerine Trip.